THE LEFT SEAT

Avoid the Turbulence on Your Journey to Becoming a Licensed Pilot

ADRIANNE FLEMING

First published by Ultimate World Publishing 2021
Copyright © 2021 Adrianne Fleming

ISBN

Paperback: 978-1-922497-74-1
Ebook: 978-1-922497-75-8

Adrianne Fleming has asserted her rights under the Copyright, Designs and Patents Act 1988 to be identified as the author of this work. The information in this book is based on the author's experiences and opinions. The publisher specifically disclaims responsibility for any adverse consequences which may result from use of the information contained herein. Permission to use information has been sought by the author. Any breaches will be rectified in further editions of the book.

All rights reserved. No part of this publication may be reproduced, stored in or introduced into a retrieval system, or transmitted in any form, or by any means (electronic, mechanical, photocopying, recording or otherwise) without the prior written permission of the author. Any person who does any unauthorised act in relation to this publication may be liable to criminal prosecution and civil claims for damages. Enquiries should be made through the publisher.

Cover design: Ultimate World Publishing
Layout and typesetting: Ultimate World Publishing
Editor: Isabelle Russell
Cover image: jannoon028-Shutterstock.com

Ultimate World Publishing
Diamond Creek,
Victoria Australia 3089
www.writeabook.com.au

BOOK DEDICATION

I dedicate this book to my family.

To my Mum, who never doubted that I would achieve my dream to be a pilot.

To my husband, Geoff, thank you for believing in me and for your unwavering encouragement and support and sharing this amazing journey with me.

To my children, Matthew, Alexander and Rachael, you are my inspiration. May you follow your dreams as I did mine and live a life of happiness and abundance.

TESTIMONIALS

"Adrianne's skills as an instructor are great. She has the ability to demonstrate and break down things into simple, easy to understand instructions for her students. Her dedication and patience were prevalent, enabling me to achieve my dream of becoming a commercial pilot."

Ian Appleby
CPL

"Pilot Adrianne Fleming OAM is a passionate advocate for general aviation in Australia. She was an industry leader working for regulatory reform and innovation, and she promotes Australia internationally as a leading provider of pilot training. She has been the Executive Commissioner of the Australian Air League, encouraging young Australians to participate in aviation. *The Left Seat* is Adrianne's latest contribution to Australian aviation, and I am delighted to recommend it to anyone interested in becoming a pilot."

The Hon Gordon Rich-Phillips, MP
Shadow Minister for Aviation
Minister for Aviation 2010-2014

"Adrianne began her aviation career in 1989 at Moorabbin Aviation Academy. As her Chief Flying instructor, I supervised her training and conducted her Grade 3 Instructor Rating Flight test in January 1993. More recently, I issued Adrianne with her Flight Examiner Rating for the issue of Flight Instructor Ratings. Through the 30-odd years I have known her, Adrianne has always displayed her passion for training and has made significant contribution to the quality of pilot training. I congratulate her on this latest contribution."

Phil Betts
CASA Flight Testing Examiner

CONTENTS

The Left Seat: Introduction	1
Chapter 1: Up, Up and Away - The Framework	3
Chapter 2: Earning Your Wings - The Private Pilot Licence (PPL)	11
Chapter 3: The Short and the Long of it - The 150-hour Integrated Commercial Pilot Licence (CPL)	23
Chapter 4: The Long and the Short of it - the 200-hour Commercial Pilot Licence (CPL)	37
Chapter 5: Aeroplane Spotting - Aeroplane Types	49
Chapter 6: Know What You Are Looking For - Ratings and Endorsements	61
Chapter 7: When There is Turbulence - Barriers	75
Chapter 8: Fasten Your Seatbelt - The Airline Transport Pilot Licence (ATPL)	83
Chapter 9: Who Are You Going to Call? Choosing a Flight School	93
Chapter 10: Light Winds and Clear Skies - Enjoy the Journey	105

Chapter 11: Stay in Control – Safety	117
Chapter 12: From the Classroom to the Sky - Aviation VET in School	123
Afterword	129
Chapter 13: Bonus chapter: A Global Opportunity - International Students	131
Speaker Bio	141
Conclusion	143
Pricing Template	142
Further Testimonials	153
About the Author	157
Useful Links	159

THE LEFT SEAT

INTRODUCTION

If you have ever thought about learning to fly an aeroplane but didn't know where to start, this is the book for you. Flying is something that people often think about at a young age and then life gets in the way. Whether it be study, career or family, there are a multitude of reasons that prevent people from taking the step to learn how to fly. Sometimes, it can be as simple as not knowing where to start.

I have dedicated many hours of my life explaining to interested flyers how to go about learning to fly, and offering advice based on my experience as to the best pathway for them to take. Aviation is an exciting industry and there are lots of passionate people within it. It has its own dictionary of terms which, for the novice, can become confusing and overwhelming, making it hard to navigate and find the way that would best suit.

That is why I decided to write this book. I have seen people take the wrong path because they didn't realise there was any other way, and it has cost them considerable time and money. I have also seen people put off flying initially because of a significant other who just doesn't understand how it works and, instead of encouragement, they pass on negativity. This book is for you, or them, as it gives an outline of how the licensing system works in Australia and the different options that are available to anyone wishing to obtain a pilot licence. Much of this information can be obtained from searching on Google and various websites, but to save you the trouble I have put it together in the one place.

The information I am providing is by no means exhaustive, but I want it to be a starting point for your research into becoming a pilot. You may have waited a long time to arrive at this realisation of making your dream come true and I want to ensure that you have the answers, or are armed with the right questions, to make this journey as wonderful as it possibly can be.

To date, I have built up over 30 years of experience in this industry and still enjoy it just as much as when I first started. This could be the beginning of the most amazing journey in your life. As someone once said to me, "Be brave and embrace the opportunity." If flying is your dream, you can make it happen, and reading this book will take you that next step closer to achieving your dream.

CHAPTER 1

UP, UP AND AWAY – THE FRAMEWORK

Congratulations, you have made the first step on the journey to becoming a licensed pilot. It is likely a world that you are unfamiliar with, and it may feel a little intimidating at first. That is why I have broken up this book into easy to read chapters to inform you about the different options available to gaining a pilot's licence. This book will focus on flying fixed wing aeroplanes.

I have spoken to thousands of people just like you who have expressed interest in becoming a pilot, whether it's been a lifelong ambition, a career change, a way in which to overcome their fear of flying and even a lost bet with a friend. Whatever their initial reason may be, they owe it to themselves to do their homework and find out about the process and which options will suit them best.

There is an old joke: "How do you find a pilot at a bar? You don't have to, they will tell you."

The Left Seat

Along with telling you, there will often be a series of terminologies and pilot jargon that you have no idea how to interpret. That's why I will endeavour to expand the acronyms when they are first mentioned to minimise any confusion.

Let's start with the most common question I receive in my email inbox.

"I want to be a pilot, can you give me some information please?" Great, I say to myself, now how can I sign them up and extract their dollars… no, I'm only joking, of course that's not what I do. However, it is easy for someone to be sucked into the sales vortex of learning to fly and not know much at all. Before they know it they are thousands of dollars out of pocket and heading towards something they didn't really want or need. So, make sure you read all the chapters to avoid this happening to you.

Now, back to my email. My response after thanking them for their enquiry is often, "How much do you know about the pilot licence?" In 80% of responses, the person will not know very much at all, but sometimes they will rattle off the acronyms PPL (Private Pilot Licence) or CPL (Commercial Pilot Licence). Not knowing these at this early stage in your journey is normal, and as you read through the chapters you will become more confident with what is needed and what questions to ask as you gather your information. First, you need to understand the system of licensing before we delve further into the various types of licence.

As a flight instructor, I explain to my students that flying lessons are like a series of bricks. Each time you master a sequence you receive another brick, then gradually you put the bricks together to make a house. You need to make sure each of those bricks are of good quality as any one poor quality brick could cause the house to come crashing down.

The brick-building starts now so you can get the house, well, pilot licence, you are looking for.

The Australian System

This book will speak about the Australian system of pilot training. However, I will address the regime if you are coming from overseas in the bonus chapter.

Aviation in Australia is regulated by the Civil Aviation Safety Authority (CASA). Flight training schools, charter companies, airlines and even the ever-increasing drone operators are a few of the organisations that come under CASA's regulatory banner.

The pilot licence you eventually obtain will be issued by CASA.

There are a number of self-regulated organisations that also answer to CASA, such at the Hang Gliding Federation of Australia (HGFA), and Recreation Aviation Australia (RAAus). These organisations regulate their members and report to CASA. RAAus is a growing sector of the aviation industry looking after those flying light aircraft with two seats or less.

CASA also approve Designated Medical Examiners (DAME) who you will need to visit to determine your medical fitness for flying. We will cover more on this in a later chapter.

Flying Training - The Licence Basics

All student pilots unless in the military will start off in the General Aviation (GA) sector. GA covers a range of civil aviation operations that are not commercial air transport. Flying training fits into the GA space along with other activities such as gliding, balloon flying aeromedical services and air shows.

You have decided to learn to fly but are still unsure what type of licence you need, so let's go through the basics of the various licences. Each of these will be explained in more depth later.

The Left Seat

Stage one is the Recreational Pilot Licence (RPL). This licence is unique to Australia. When I started flying it was called the Restricted Pilot Licence - funnily enough, the same acronym. It was a Private Pilot Licence (PPL) with an area restriction. In the 90s, it went through a transformation where it was called a General Flying Progress Test (GFPT) and this time, the student pilot held a passenger carrying endorsement and an endorsement to fly single engine aeroplanes weighing no more than 5700 kilograms.

The regulatory structure may have changed a few times, but the basic permissions are similar.

All of these variations did the same thing by allowing a person to fly an aeroplane in the local area, departing and arriving at the same aerodrome and being able to carry passengers. I only mention this because sometimes people, in their quest to find out how to get a licence, which I wholeheartedly encourage, get confused because they have been speaking with a person who has a pilot licence but may have completed it under the earlier system.

Stage two is the PPL. The PPL is universal around the world, and the training for the RPL does form part of the global PPL syllabus. After obtaining a PPL, you are able to fly with passengers across the country as you are no longer limited to the local area.

The PPL is for private flying, where you are able to take friends and family flying to any destination, any time. This is not the licence you require if you wish to work as a pilot. However, just as the training you did in the RPL led you toward your PPL, the training you conduct in the PPL stage of your flying is part of the lead-in training toward your Commercial Pilot Licence (CPL), if that is where you wish to go.

Stage three is the CPL, the licence you require if you wish to work "for hire or reward" as a pilot. The training that you completed in the PPL stage is part of the preparation you will need to have before gaining a

CPL. There are many ways to achieve the CPL and these will be discussed in detail in later chapters to enable you to make an informed choice.

The Air Transport Pilot Licence (ATPL) is the licence you require to be a captain in an aircraft with a higher weight category. Think of when you board an aeroplane at the airport for your interstate or international flight. The pilot up the front with the four bars on their uniform sitting in the left seat is the captain who holds an ATPL.

There are additional endorsements and ratings that can be put onto each of the licences which are explained in greater detail in a later chapter. Aviation is a highly regulated industry and becoming a pilot means you will be subjected to learning many rules. One of the qualities listed for a pilot is the ability to understand technical information, so you can start here with a little bit of information on airspace and airports.

Australian Airports and Airspace

Australia has been involved in aviation from the pioneer days, and the sheer size of the country lends itself to an active aviation industry. In basic terms, there are two types of airspace: controlled and uncontrolled. Controlled is where there is some form of interaction between pilot and Air Traffic Control (ATC) needed to operate in the airspace. Whereas in uncontrolled airspace, pilots follow certain procedures without any ATC intervention. Due to Australia's size, the controlled airspace is around capital city airports, usually described as an upside-down wedding cake, getting wider as it goes higher.

Airports are also classified to indicate which procedures and control requirements are needed to operate in it. Each capital city has a major airport where most of the domestic and international airlines operate in and out of.

The Left Seat

Many of the capital cities also have a smaller airport with an ATC tower. The following airports have been specifically set up for training, as it would be difficult for pilots to train at major city airports:

Melbourne – Moorabbin Airport

Sydney – Bankstown and Camden Airports

Brisbane – Archerfield Airport

Adelaide – Parafield Airport

Perth – Jandakot Airport

Hobart – Cambridge Airport

These airports have several flight schools and aviation companies operating out of them. There is a good chance that if you are from one of these capital cities, you will learn to fly from one of these airports.

Further out of the major cities there are other smaller airports where flying training also occurs. These airports may be privately owned or operated by local councils. Many regional centres across Australia have regularly active airports.

Once you hold a PPL, you will be licensed to fly in all types of airspace and in and out of all categories of airports across Australia.

Now, that wasn't too bad, was it? It does get a little more technical, but you already have the basics. You are reading this book because you want to become a pilot. As you will learn there is more than one way to become a pilot. There are options to train as a pilot, and at the same time gain an academic qualification along the way, although none of the academic qualifications are mandatory to obtain the CASA licence. Think of them as an optional extra, and like most extras, they are likely to cost you extra time and money.

Academic Qualifications

In more recent times, additional academic qualifications have been introduced which you can obtain whilst undergoing your CPL training. Part of your CASA pilot licence studies count for partial credit towards these. The licence is still issued by CASA and the academic qualification, depending on what it is, will be issued by the institute. Some flight schools have partnered with a university to offer a Bachelor of Aviation as the academic qualification along with the CASA CPL.

There are also flight schools offering the Diploma of Aviation with a CPL. The flight school needs to be a Registered Training Organisation (RTO) registered with the Australian Skills Quality Authority (ASQA) to offer the academic award of the diploma. This registration is additional to their CASA approvals to train pilots for the CPL. The Diploma of Aviation may also be offered through some TAFE colleges and utilising a flight school as a third party provider.

Now you have a better idea of the framework, let's find out more on the actual licence processes.

CHAPTER 2

EARNING YOUR WINGS – THE PRIVATE PILOT LICENCE (PPL)

Now you understand a little bit about the system, this chapter will discuss the PPL.

A PPL is one of the steps towards obtaining a CPL, so even if you are not sure whether you wish to train to be a commercial pilot, you can change your mind along the way, and the flying experience you gain will never be wasted.

Throughout this chapter, I will concentrate on the nitty-gritty small things that you need to do to obtain a PPL. The first thing to remember is that a PPL is a licence for fun. It is where you don't have the commercial pressures associated with your flights. After qualifying, you fly when and where you want. Most people who dream about flying will find that a PPL is something that they really enjoy having. It's not a job. It is something that they do for leisure.

The Left Seat

Let's take a look at what's involved and how you can most efficiently complete your PPL. The PPL can be divided into two stages the RPL (stage one) and then the PPL (stage two). You're not required to complete the RPL flight test on the way to a PPL, but my experience has shown that it's really good benchmark for people to achieve that first milestone.

The syllabus of the RPL is where you will start. When you look at the hours for a RPL whilst you make enquiries at different flying schools, what you are likely to see published is the price for the minimum hours required. Now, the minimum hours are set by the aviation regulator. The Civil Aviation Safety Authority state that the minimum hours for a RPL is 25 hours. Within those 25 hours, a minimum of 5 hours solo and 20 hours dual. What does solo mean? Solo is where there is only one person in the aeroplane. Dual flight hours are those accumulated when you are under training with the flight instructor in the aircraft with you.

The average flight lesson for the RPL stage is one hour in the aeroplane there is also a briefing with the instructor pre- and post-flight. The minimum hours of 25 does not provide much experience if you compare with what is required to gain a drivers licence. In my many years of instructing I have known very few people who have completed all their training within the minimum hours. On average, giving yourself a budget for 35 hours would be more realistic. There are lots of variables when conducting flying training for any licence. You could have two people training at the same school with the same instructor on the same day, and they each experience different weather conditions, and different traffic conditions, different runway configurations. All these differences can make it difficult to predict timings on when a student will be competent at the skills being taught. Flying is an individual sport, with the skills taught one-on-one with an instructor in the aeroplane. The only person you are competing with is yourself.

Earning Your Wings - The Private Pilot Licence (PPL)

Knowledge is important

It's a common perception that pilots need to be good at math and physics. In reality, it doesn't hurt, but it's not a deal breaker if you find yourself in the humanities stream instead. The real issue is that no one wants a dumb pilot, and we will talk more about academics in chapter 7. The first theory course of study you will need to complete is the RPL theory. Once you are confident with all the content, you will take the RPL theory exam. The exam is online, and generally it can be taken at the flight school, or at an exam center.

Most people don't like exams, me included, however think of the reward for passing - getting the opportunity to go flying. Some of the topics covered in the RPL theory course are general rules of the air, aerodynamics, where you learn how an aeroplane can fly, meteorology and local weather forecasts. Human factors are covered from the beginning of a pilot's training, as they are important for a pilot to understand how behavior and performance can affect the safe outcome of a flight. It is not only human performance that is studied; aircraft performance is of equal importance. If I had an aeroplane and I filled it up with as much fuel as the tanks would take, then I filled the baggage compartment with as many bags as could possibly fit, that aeroplane is now potentially too heavy to take off. So, not only would that aeroplane not be able to take off, but it might also run out of runway length trying to do so. Obviously, this is not a desirable situation, which is why it is important to study aircraft performance so the pilot can make adjustments beforehand to conduct a safe flight and prevent any accident.

Another topic covered is aircraft engines and systems. If the thought of studying this or any other of the subjects scares you, don't let it, as most of the theory textbooks make the information quite simple to understand. It is important as a pilot to have some knowledge of the machine you are operating. We're a lot more vigilant with our aeroplanes than we are with our cars. Every time before we go flying, we complete a preflight inspection, during which the pilot will walk around the aircraft and check how much fuel and oil is in the aeroplane, and if there are any contaminants in the fuel. The pilot will also look at the fuselage, check all the lights are working, and see if the tyres are inflated sufficiently. I doubt many people, almost none, would do that in their cars. This is part of the discipline of becoming a pilot and something you cannot compromise on.

See, Feel and Do - The Recreational Pilot Licence (RPL)

A flying instructor is taught to brief a student before the flight on what they will see, feel and do. I will apply this same philosophy in each of the licence stages.

I mentioned that in the RPL, each lesson is approximately an hour long. A student who attends the flight school for their lesson will undertake a pre-flight brief with the flight instructor on what sequence they will be undertaking in that lesson. The student may have had some homework prior to the flight. I recommend that if you want to maximise the time you spend in the aeroplane, make sure you do all the homework the instructor gives you prior to the flight. Catching up and learning on the go can be an expensive way to gain your licence. Now, with that in mind, I will now discuss the lessons. The early lessons build on one another: how to climb the plane, fly the plane in a straight line, how to descend and turn. Then you get to put those lessons all together in the circuit pattern where you will learn to take off and land the aeroplane. Once you have passed some knowledge questions and are competent to take off and land, your instructor will allow you to experience one of the most memorable moments in your life: your first solo flight. This usually consists of one circuit all by yourself - yes, solo, with no one looking over your shoulder. Your instructor will be watching from the side of the runway.

I can still recall my first solo, as will any pilot. I was not used to wearing a headset as quite a few of my lessons simply used a hand microphone. If you are using a headset, there is a small button on the controls that you push down to transmit your radio call. Needless to say, I was fairly excited about the prospect of flying a plane all by myself. When the air traffic controller cleared me for take-off, I pushed the button and responded with, "Clear for take-off," and my aircraft call sign but instead of releasing the button after those words my finger stayed on it a little longer and the transmission included my little self-talk: "Well, Adrianne, you are on your own now." At this point, I was lined up on the runway and about to take off. I realised my finger was still pushed down and quickly released it to hear the air traffic controller humorously say, "You certainly are, good luck." Other than that slight oversight, the flight went well.

All going well on your solo flight, you will then complete subsequent solo circuit flights and return to dual lessons of more advanced manoeuvres covering emergency landing, steep turns for co-ordination and more advanced circuits. During this time, you will have also completed a theory course and taken the RPL theory examination. There is additional solo flying to practice the more advanced manoeuvres and finally a pre-licence check with your instructor, and if they think you are competent, they will recommend you for a flight check with an examiner.

Now, the flight test for the RPL is the first one that you will ever do. This can be a little daunting, this is totally natural because it will be your first time in the flight test environment. The challenge is to ensure you focus on what is required on the day. Flight tests are never easy, but after the first one you are more aware of what to expect and how you perform in the test environment. The RPL flight test consists of theory questions verbally asked by the examiner, some performance data for the flight and a flight of around one-and-a-half hours, covering the items you have been trained in. On successful completion of your flight test, you will be granted your RPL, although you cannot use this until you have received a copy in the mail from CASA.

The Left Seat

Now, you have your RPL, let's share the joy.
You can now carry passengers and fly them around the local area. The term "joy flight" is apt as this is what you and your passengers are now able to experience. Unlike commercial joy flights, you are not being paid for the flight, although you can share the cost of the aircraft hire for your flight equally amongst yourself and passengers. This is called "cost share".

The RPL allows you to carry passengers in the aircraft, and you can fly them around the local area within 25 nautical miles from the departure aerodrome. There may be some additional limitations on where you can fly from certain aerodromes due to the proximity of various airspace types nearby. You will become familiar with any of these during your training. If you decided to hire an aircraft from a different flight school at a different airport the flight school is likely to assist you with this local knowledge in their check flight. Different types of airspace and aerodromes can require different endorsements additional to your initial RPL.

Let's talk about those endorsements. An RPL gives you the ability to add different endorsements. I said you could travel within 25 nautical miles, which is because in those 25 hours, you've learned to fly the aeroplane. You've learned to take it off, land, and fly around the local area with the local flying procedures. You haven't yet learned to navigate. In some airports, you may not have an air traffic control tower. So, you may not have learned the radio procedures that are required for an air traffic controlled airport. If you did not initially train to do any of these additional items they can be added onto the privileges of the RPL with some specific training.

Additional Endorsements
The navigation endorsement will teach you how to navigate so you are not limited to the 25 nautical miles from the departure aerodrome. This consists of a minimum of five hours solo cross country flying with two hours dual instrument flying. There are the controlled

Earning Your Wings – The Private Pilot Licence (PPL)

aerodrome and controlled airspace endorsements which, as they suggest, allow you to fly at an aerodrome that has an ATC tower or in airspace that is controlled by ATC. Both of these require the flight radio endorsement to enable you to use the radio to communicate. Being able to communicate when flying is important, and the flight radio endorsement also has an English language test that must be completed prior to the flight radio endorsement being issued.

If you're flying at an airport with a control tower when you gain your RPL, you will be issued a flight radio endorsement, which is registered as a controlled aerodrome endorsement on your RPL. You need all of these so that you can operate from that airport.

There is no time limit on how quickly you should proceed to a PPL after completing a RPL. There is also no requirement to proceed any further than the RPL. However, like any of the pilot licences, it does require validation every two years. This procedure is called a flight review which will be completed with a qualified flight instructor.

The Private Pilot Licence (PPL)

The next stage of licence is the PPL. If you hold an RPL (some people may decide not to complete the RPL flight test) the PPL is the part that is going to teach you how to navigate. The navigation endorsement on the RPL is one option however there is no need to complete this if you plan on completing your PPL. The full PPL will cover the syllabus items in all the RPL endorsements which is why many people continue on to the PPL rather than gaining the separate RPL navigation endorsement.

More Theory
The PPL phase of training includes another theory examination. This examination is online too and can be taken at most flight schools or an exam centre. There are four key subjects that make up the

PPL theory course of study: Human factors (which you should have already studied in the RPL), meteorology which is an extension on what was studied for the RPL, flight rules & air law and navigation are the subjects that would have the most additional content. When you think of theory required for flying don't think of it as something you learn for an exam and then forget. Aviation theory is generally quite practical and has a visible purpose. The theory that you would have covered in the RPL phase is a good foundation to build upon in the PPL phase.

The PPL – See, Feel and Do

You know how to fly a plane, but you need to learn how to navigate. The second stage or PPL is another 20 hours. Those 20 hours are going to consist of 15 hours of dual flying, and 5 hours of solo flying. This could also be broken down further into eight navigation exercises: 6 dual and 2 solo.

Before your first navigation exercise there will be a significant amount of time that you will need to spend in the classroom. This time will be spent planning. We've heard about the five Ps: Prior Planning Prevents Poor Performance. These are invaluable to conducting a well-executed navigation exercise, particularly in the early navigation exercises when everything is new. Before you learn how to complete a flight plan, you need to have an understanding on how to obtain and check the weather forecast. There is a significant amount of theory knowledge required before a person completes a flight plan. So, it makes sense that PPL students have completed the PPL theory course prior to starting the PPL training. It can be completed concurrently with the flying, however it is generally easier if the theory course is completed prior, as many of the concepts are utilised in the actual navigation sequences.

You will learn how to draw lines on a map, measure the distances, and interpret weather forecast and wind information to calculate the headings required to keep the aircraft on track and calculate how much fuel is required to complete the flight. Once you have calculated all

Earning Your Wings - The Private Pilot Licence (PPL)

this information, you will add the relevant information into a flight plan and learn how to submit the plan so that ATC have your details.

When you learn to fly in the RPL phase, it is a step-by-step approach. You learn one sequence, and another sequence, and then another and each one will build upon the previous. This is the same approach when you complete the navigation phase of your training. The training starts with a short relatively simple navigation exercise (navex), then the next navex will be longer and more complex, however you will be completing the same sequences at different locations. This repetition aids in learning how to navigate.

When your instructor feels that you are competent in navigating, they will authorise you to complete a navigation exercise on your own. Similar to your first solo, you are likely to remember that first solo navex where the reality of what having a pilot licence is all about is realised. After the solo navex, you will complete more dual navexes increasing your confidence and competence and another longer solo navex. Then it is time for your pre-licence flight, which is completed with the instructor. All licences have a pre-licence check with an instructor to put you through your paces. If you are found competent in the pre-licence navex, you will be recommended for a flight test with an examiner. The flight test follows the similar format as the RPL. You will have been given a flight plan to complete a couple of days earlier, so you can have everything planned for the flight. Then, on the day, you will adjust for the relevant weather conditions. The examiner will ask you theory questions on the ground and you will then take the examiner on the planned navigation flight, just as if you were taking a friend or family member flying.

Upon completion of a successful PPL flight test, you will be issued with a PPL. Passing the PPL test, you will be able to fly wherever you desire across Australia, other than restricted areas - but you are unlikely to want to go there anyway. Just like your RPL, you cannot use the PPL until you have received the actual licence from CASA.

Going Places

What can you do with a PPL? With a PPL your new vehicle of choice is an aeroplane. You can fly from A to B, around the country, during daylight hours only. If you want to learn to fly at night, there are additional ratings such as the night VFR or instrument rating you must add on. We'll talk about these in chapter 6.

Let's talk about one of the many pleasures of having a pilot licence. John is a doctor, and he uses his PPL to fly to his practice in rural areas of Australia. He lives in a major city and his clinic is also based in the city. Once every two weeks, he has a clinic in a regional part of the state, and instead of getting in his car and driving to the hospital, he drives to the airport in the morning, gets in his plane, and instead of it taking him almost four hours to drive to this regional hospital, it will only take him just over an hour-and-a-half to fly.

John utilises the aeroplane as just as he would his car, as his transport backwards and forwards to his regional clinic. There are several doctors that do this. However, flying is not just for doctors. Let us look at some other examples of how the PPL can be used. Sarah has a PPL, and endeavours to fly as often as she can on weekends. She has a group of friends she takes once a month to a different location for a weekend away. With the blessing of good weather, Sarah takes her friends to a country town usually within two hours' flying distance, which would normally be approximately four hours driving time. Sarah and her friends spend time away for the weekend then they fly back on Sunday afternoon before it gets dark so they can all get back for work on Monday.

I mentioned the term "cost share" earlier in regards to the RPL. Sarah's flight was a total of four hours: two hours there, two hours back. If you divide the cost amongst Sarah and the three passengers, they would each be paying for an hour aircraft hire. That makes for quite an affordable weekend for Sarah and her friends.

Earning Your Wings – The Private Pilot Licence (PPL)

A quick note on aircraft hire. I am often asked by prospective pilots, "If I take an aeroplane away for a week, am I paying for every hour the plane is away?' The answer is no, generally you will hire the aeroplane and you'll pay only while the engine's running. So, if you take it away for seven days, but you are only flying there and back, you are not paying for the time the aircraft is not running. There may be a parking fee at the aerodrome, but it is only the engine running time you pay for just as with Sarah and her friends.

Now, Sarah is a pilot who tries to fly as often as she can. Another question I am often asked is, "Do I have to fly all the time to keep my licence?" I briefly mentioned earlier that a flight review is required every 2 years to validate your licence. Other than this there is no minimum hours mandated that you must fly in that two-year period. Common sense is left to prevail on competency and many flight schools have an insurance requirement that can vary from 30 to 90-day dual checks with an instructor. There is a requirement for the carriage of passengers: if you wish to carry passengers, you must complete three take-offs and landings in the last 90 days. This rule applies for the RPL, PPL and CPL.

For example, if you have a licence but you haven't flown for six months, it's still valid. But if you want to carry passengers, you are going to have to either go up with an instructor and complete the three take-offs and landings, or hire an aeroplane by yourself and do three take-offs and landings, then if all goes well, and you are generally competent, you meet the requirements to take up the passengers.

Learning to fly while at school is cool

This chapter has focused on the RPL and PPL and what each of the licences entail. Learning to fly as part of your schooling is another option for some students. When I was at school, the closest I ever came to studying aviation was looking out the window as a plane flew overhead. This is no longer the case as many students have the opportunity to study to become a pilot as part of their school curriculum. I currently train several secondary students in Years 11 and 12 under the Vocational Education and Training (VET) system, more in chapter 12. These students are training for the RPL and completing the theory training towards a Diploma in Aviation. A bonus with flying theory is that it puts all those school subjects to work. So, often students at school will say, "Why am I doing geography? What is the point of that math equation?" Learning the theory associated with gaining a pilot's licence helps you put practical applications to many of the theoretical concepts taught at school. For students who are looking at a career as a pilot or in the aviation industry, this is a great option for them to get a head start. Flying solo before you can drive a car embeds a strong sense of self-discipline and personal maturity in the individual student.

Recreational Pilot Certificate
I mentioned earlier about Recreational Aviation Australia (RAAus) where there are restrictions on the size of the aircraft, the number of passengers, medical requirements, and airspace. These are potential advantages for many, and it is a large and growing area in the industry. RAAus has the Recreational Pilot Certificate (RPC), which shares some similarities to the RPL. The RPC pilot can upgrade with a navigation endorsement or can also upgrade to an RPL. The RPC is sometimes confused with the RPL particularly for the beginner, which is why I mention it here because they are different. There are flight schools that can offer both the RPL and RPC as they have both approvals.

CHAPTER 3

THE SHORT AND THE LONG OF IT - THE 150-HOUR INTEGRATED COMMERCIAL PILOT LICENCE (CPL)

In the many years that I have been out advertising my business or working in my business, people will say to me, "I want to complete a CPL." To enable me to understand what I need to explain I'll reply with, "Do you understand how the CPL course works?" Their response is usually "yes." So, my next question is, "Are you planning on completing the integrated or non-integrated course?" It's after this question that they then stare at me blankly.

It is important, as I will keep saying throughout this book, that you do your homework. A CPL is a significant investment in both time and finances; there is much to know. This chapter is going to talk about the integrated course, or the 150-hour CPL course. Internationally, ICAO set a standard CPL at 200 hours, and then an integrated course has a reduction in hours to 150. If you're planning on completing a

The Left Seat

150-hour integrated course, you will have to do this at a flight school that has a Part 142 approval. Flight schools issued with a Part 142 approval from CASA have the ability to reduce the Commercial Pilot Licence course from 200 hours to 150 hours.

You can confirm whether the flight school is a Part 142 when you make your enquiry to the school. The Civil Aviation Safety Authority www.casa.gov.au also provides a search check on their website.

What is the Breakdown of These Hours?

The flight test you need to pass at the end of a CPL course is the same whether it's a 200-hour or a 150-hour course. The candidate must meet the same competency requirements of a commercial pilot. Anytime the CPL flight test is completed prior to 200 hours, you must be on a 150-hour course. The concept of an integrated course is that from zero up to the flight test is completed smoothly and the flight school has from day one right down to the last day all planned. Each of the flight and theory hours you take in the 150-hour course is part of an integrated, scheduled programme. It is the scheduled nature of the course that allows for the reduction in hours.

The breakdown of hours in the 150-hour integrated course requires a minimum of 70 hours of flight time as Pilot in Command (PIC). The remainder of the hours are usually scheduled with an instructor, however this can vary between flight schools. The 70-hour PIC is a mandatory requirement. The flight school will look at how they can achieve all the competencies in the syllabus in that minimum amount of time.

If you enrol in a CPL course, you will still have to complete the competencies for the PPL and the RPL. However, depending on the course, you may not be required to take both of these licence flight tests. Some flight schools may choose to only do one of either the RPL

The Short and the long of It

or PPL flight test, and then the CPL test. Other flight schools could have all the three flight tests in their syllabus. As an examiner, I am yet to meet anyone who enjoys a flight test, however, completing each of the flight tests is a good benchmark for the stages of your learning and gives you that sense of achievement along the way.

The CPL integrated 150-hour course is the quickest way in which you can achieve a CPL, in the minimum hours. The theory requirements and skill requirements for the CPL are the same regardless of whether you are enrolled in the 150-hour or 200-hour CPL course. There is no reduction in theory requirements, only flying hours in the integrated course.

In the PPL chapter I spoke about the theory and exam required for both the RPL and PPL. The theory for the PPL phase of the licence covered navigation, human factors, meteorology, and air law, you will find similar subjects as part of the CPL theory. In fact, meteorology, and human factors, are likely to be very similar. Navigation is expanded to build on what you have already learnt, and the air law will cover rules as they relate to commercial operations. Additional subjects are operations performance and flight planning, aerodynamics and aircraft general knowledge (AGK). These too will expand on the knowledge you learnt whilst studying your RPL and PPL. Depending on your course the similar subjects may be studied concurrently.

Any theory exam for the respective licences must be passed before you take the flight test. The pass mark for most of those theory exams is 70%. This is something I wasn't aware of before I started flying training. So, if you were thinking that 50% is good enough and you just skim over the lines of the knowledge, you will need to raise the bar for aviation. You need to make 70% as a minimum your new norm and for the air law exams, it is 80%. For many, a result of 70% on an exam is considered okay, however in aviation you will still be verbally asked and tested on the 30% that you didn't answer correctly. This may seem pedantic but, if you think about it, that 30%

of missing knowledge in aviation may be something that is actually critical to safety. That is why it is important for you to achieve the 100% knowledge standard.

The Steps to CPL

For the early sequences of the 150-hour CPL you will complete the syllabus for the RPL and PPL. First learning how to fly the aeroplane, then after the RPL, you will learn how to navigate the aeroplane. It is after you have either completed the PPL or are competent at navigation you will then commence gaining command time. Command time is where you complete a series of navigation exercises flying from one place to another gaining experience. This command time is where pilots practice and develop their flying skills and confidence which they will take to the commercial phase of flying training. Within the 150-hour integrated course, the flight school will have carefully planned a set of navigation routes as part of the syllabus for your command time. There may be some minor alterations due to weather, but these are the routes you shall take to achieve the maximum amount of experience in the minimum amount of time.

If you passed a PPL flight test as part of the integrated CPL you are licensed to carry passengers, where you can take them on a flight away for the weekend. However, generally, inside the 150-hour course, you will not be permitted to count these hours towards the 70 hours in command required for the CPL. This is because the command time forms part of the course with the set navigation routes as required by the flight school's syllabus. You may be able to hire an aircraft outside of your course and complete a flight. However, it's unlikely it will be counted towards that 70 hours of command time that you require as part of the course. If you are not sure, ask the flight school.

Ideally, the purpose of the integrated course is to complete your flying training in a shorter period of time. Integrating the theory and

The Short and the long of It

flying to create efficiencies giving the CPL candidate a reduction in hours. Even though there is no regulatory cap on time frame for the integrated course, most courses are scheduled between 48 weeks to 18 months full-time. In this short time period you have to learn all the theory subjects with a 70%, and sometimes 80%, pass mark, and complete the skills based flying competencies to become a commercial pilot. Flying training is adult learning, you need to be dedicated and ensure you attend your classes, because if you miss something, there's not a lot of time allowed to catch up. I sometimes say, "Imagine if I gave you a fire hose and put it to your mouth and said drink." There is a huge amount of knowledge you need to take in and there will be bits you can't necessarily absorb in the first take. That is why it is important that you study hard and make use of all your time to ensure you make up for the information spills. If you work diligently and follow the directions of your instructor, you should be able to successfully make it to the 150-hour CPL end game.

A Diploma or Degree

The course I have described is all the CASA requirements for the CPL. However, you will often find the course may be attached to a diploma or a degree course. The diploma or the degree adds a formal academic qualification to the CASA CPL course. The academic requirements are additional to what is required for CASA. There will be separate assessments for the diploma and degree subjects. The duration of the course will vary when the additional academic qualifications are added. Diploma courses are offered by flight schools that are also a Registered Training Organisation and the degree courses will be offered by a university that has its own flight school or partner flight training provider.

If you enrol in an aviation degree course this will give you access to the government HECS loan. Paying it off regularly like any loan will minimise the debt. The VET Student Loan (VSL) system is available for some of the diploma courses. Remember, your VSL or your HECS loan is a loan, and you will have to pay it back at a later date. Another option is to pay for the course out of your own pocket as you complete the course to minimise the additional fees.

A common question I am often asked is, "Do I need a degree to get into an airline?" Currently, in Australia, there is no requirement for you to have a degree. However, the airline world is competitive, and you may find if somebody has a degree and somebody doesn't have a degree and the rest of their qualifications are equal, the degree might put them slightly ahead. That requirement rests with the airline to decide when they're recruiting. Recruiting material does not specifically state the requirement for a degree. The airline cadet programmes also do not involve a degree. I hear you ask, "Do the airlines require a diploma?" None of them state that either.

If you want or feel the need to attend university to obtain a degree, ensure you complete something that will compliment your skill set with the investment you are making. You may not always be able to fly, for instance if there is a temporary medical setback or a slowdown in the industry. It can be good to diversify in this instance. I know of several students who have completed non-aviation degrees and during that same three years in their down time have also managed to complete a CPL course. In this instance, the CPL course has been completed part-time around their university schedule.

The Cadet Pilot Course

You might be looking at a Cadet Pilot Course, so let's discuss it further. A Cadet Pilot Course is one where you have been recruited by the airline. The airline will complete a series of aptitude tests and interviews to determine whether you are suitable. If selected, you will be given a letter of intent to employ you. This is not an offer of employment. Provided that the airline needs pilots and you complete the course successfully, and then you pass through the airline's induction course and training. There are no guarantees, however, if successful it is likely the quickest pathway to becoming an airline pilot.

In a cadet course, you'll generally find, (and we're not going to talk specific prices here) that a cadet course is more expensive. It does have the likelihood that you will be employed by an airline on completion but this is not a guarantee. At the beginning of 2020, there was a global shortage of airline pilots. There are, and will be, downturns, however these do turn around in time and when the opportunities arise people still want to travel by air to their destinations. The population is growing and with this, more people will want to travel by air and so there will still be a need for more pilots.

Completing the 150-hour CPL course is a means in which you can obtain the CPL reasonably quickly; and the availability of airline cadet courses is the most direct option to an airline with all going well.

When I was learning to fly it was common knowledge that if you were not in an airline by the time you reached 27 you could forget it. This did generate a sense of urgency in your career progression. Times have definitely changed, and many of those people who missed out in their late twenties all those years ago have since been employed by airlines. There is not the rush there used to be so there is the luxury of taking your time to enjoy the many aspects of the piloting career.

"The New Work Smarts" study completed by the Foundation for Young Australians states that it is more likely that a 15-year-old today will experience a career portfolio potentially having 17 different jobs and over 5 careers. This does cause me to ponder the Cadet Pilot Course. Take a school leaver who has just completed secondary school, wants to be a pilot and signs up for a cadet course. They have done nothing else but go to school, and now in a period of 18 months to two years, they're going to get a CPL and enter into their first pilot job. Fantastic for them, when many of their other friends are still at university, but are they going to stay there, or are they instead going to feel the need to move jobs or change airlines? Only time will tell, but it does concern me that if people are having so many jobs, that they've invested all that money and all that time in job number one. We are talking hundreds of thousands of dollars. I have met many pilots who have started pilot training with an airline career in mind, decided along the way that it's not for them and they have very successful pilot careers outside of the airline environment. For a person who aspires to be a career pilot, the haste of the cadet course could deprive them of this possible realisation and opportunity.

I've talked about the 150-hour CPL course and the advantages of doing the course, so let's delve into some of the key issues I have come across. I believe many of these occur because the student was not prepared and well informed before they committed to the course.

When people sign up for an integrated course, they are signing up for a complete course of training. Some students find that after the first 20-30 hours it is not what they expected so they leave without completing, and unfortunately this comes with a fee. It is important to be aware of what is going to be asked of you, and if it is what you really want rather than be caught up in the excitement and glamour of becoming a pilot.

In large integrated courses, you are training with several other classmates. It is true you are only competing against yourself, but in a full-time course the flight training organisation has to deal with more than just you. To manage several students in such a short period of time requires tight organisation, often with the weather causing several changes. Remember the flying training organisation will have another batch of students ready to start when your course is completed. So there is minimal ability to deal with those who get left behind. If you do not achieve the required standard in the allocated time due to a variety of reasons, then there is not a lot of availability to reschedule. This is not to say you are incompetent, but you may not fit with the

The Short and the long of It

flow of the rest of the class. If you are unable to catch up, this may lead to you being dropped out of the course.

Integrated courses are one of the fastest ways of obtaining a CPL. See it like a conveyer belt making cookies: each part of the process is timed, baked, fit the mold and cut to perfection, there are systematic processes in place. You need to be made of the right ingredients to complete the process to the end. Most cookies make the cut, however what if you are the one that isn't the right shape or ingredients. Does this mean you are not going achieve your goal of being a pilot? No, of course not, but you need to reflect on your life so far. Consider how you have coped in a pressured learning environment and decide whether you will fit into the system.

The integrated course is designed to be quick and efficient and is relying on you to gain the required skills in a minimum number of hours. Some of the courses have aptitude tests to complete before you start the process, however this doesn't guarantee you will be able to keep up the pace of the course. If you don't keep up, it is likely to cost more money, to complete more training and of course there is the time factor. There is nothing wrong if you have the additional money and time, however when your classmates progress quicker and graduate before you do, this can affect your confidence. I understand you haven't even started flying yet, but it is important to know what could happen so you can protect yourself against any adverse effects.

Unfortunately, over the years I have encountered several candidates that didn't fit the mold. Their piloting skills are easy to fix, however their shattered confidence is much harder to repair.

A system is for the many, and if you are made of the correct ingredients, you'll progress though the system without any major issues.

What I have seen is that there are people that make good pilots but are not suited to this system - this is okay. The integrated course is just one method. Remember, a CPL test candidate must meet the competencies of the CPL flight test regardless of which system they have trained under.

Signing on the Dotted Line

When you sign up for an integrated course, be sure to understand what training you are receiving for the fees you are paying. Also check the refund policy just in case you don't fit the mold, or even if you change your mind and do not want to complete the entire course. If you have any doubts about really wanting to become a pilot, you may like to look at an alternative pathway so you are not locked in.

I have met pilot trainees that signed up for the course because they like the uniform and thought they would attract girls by becoming a pilot. You may laugh as I did, but the more important point is that any pilot trainee requires motivation. The course is not only a test of their academic ability but also their manipulative skills at the controls of the aeroplane. Together, they require hard work from the student. If your motivations are weak then perhaps a pilot course is not for you.

The integrated course you sign up for is scheduled from day one to completion day. There needs to be a little bit of flexibility because the flight school can't control the weather. If you want or need to take a break during the course, you must check what allowances are made for this and how it could affect the cost and duration of the course.

Completion Rates

With any investment in both time and money you should research the completion rates of the course you select. It is quite sad to see that compared to the amount of people who start, the amount of people who finish is significantly less. I can cite numerous graduates from

The Short and the long of It

courses across the country where less than 20% of the class they started with completed the course and are now working in the industry.

I have seen several school leavers get caught up in the excitement of being accepted into a course straight out of school. Often when at school, it is just a matter of ticking a box to say you are pursuing a pilot career with minimal research. It is not until the course has started that the realisation that flying is hard and maybe piloting isn't really for them. Whatever the reason, you don't want to be one of these non-finishers. You need to ensure you are enrolled in the course that will suit you.

It is important to understand from the start that learning to fly is hard, if it wasn't, everyone would be able to do it. It takes time to learn the skills required and you will forever be tested on those skills throughout your career. It often starts as a dream and becomes something you are passionate about, but you will have to be prepared to work hard for it.

COMMON QUESTIONS

I have answered some common questions I receive on the 150-hour integrated course. There may be more than one answer to each of the questions and it may vary between flight training courses

What happens to my flight hours if I drop out of a course?

The hours you have flown will always be in your logbook and count towards your flying time. The training you have completed similarly forms part of your experience.

I dropped out of a CPL course a few years ago, how do I go about continuing again?

As per the previous answer, the flying hours and experience you have gained stay with you. Flight training schools have different points of entry that they may credit you towards the course. Depending on the school, they may allow you to enter at a specific entry point. For example, if you have your PPL with some command flying hours completed they may let you enter the course at the point of the PPL. Common gates are first solo, RPL and PPL. Anything further than this and it is likely you may have to enrol in the non-integrated 200-hour CPL course.

I am moving interstate and need to change flight schools.

If you wish to change flight schools because of circumstances that have arisen, you can give permission for your new flight training school to transfer your training records. The new school may require you to complete an assessment flight, particularly if it is in a different location or utilises different aircraft, and then determine what they will credit as the entry point into their course.

What if I am completing an aviation degree course and want to change degree courses?

If you want to continue flying, this is possible and can be arranged with the flight training provider. For the degree change, you would discuss with the university as to what options are available in relation to changing degree courses.

If I complete the 150-hour integrated course is this going to allow me to obtain that first job quicker than completing the 200-hour course?

If you look at the programme of many of the 150-hour integrated courses you will find with the exception of the 70 hours command that is required at the point of the flight test the total hours you have are more likely around 170 hours. The difference between 170 and 200 hours is now starting to narrow and the gap in this instance is only 30 hours. A person getting 30 hours of command time by flying around the country could achieve this in a few weeks, so the time difference to holding the CPL ready for the first job can often be negligible.

We discuss the 200-hour CPL course in the next chapter.

Is there any way I can fast track the 150-hour CPL?

The 150-hour integrated course is scheduled. Remember earlier I mentioned the fire hose analogy to the amount of information that is imparted during a CPL course. Sure, if you are a quick learner and complete all your tasks to standard. The flying training is competency based and you could cut down the time in-between lessons depending on the flight school's schedule. The 150 hours are a regulatory requirement so even if you met the standard in less than this, you would still have to obtain the hours before being allowed to undertake a flight test.

The Left Seat

The 150-hour integrated CPL course is accepted as the most structured of the CPL training. On completion it will be your point of entry into the industry as a working pilot. There are additional skill-sets you can add to the CPL which may enhance your chances of employment. These are covered in chapter 6, it will depend on what pathway you are wanting to take.

CHAPTER 4

THE LONG AND THE SHORT OF IT - THE 200-HOUR COMMERCIAL PILOT LICENCE (CPL)

The CPL 200-hour syllabus is the flexible syllabus. Even though you cover the same elements of competency as in the 150-hour course, the syllabus gives you greater control over the timing, choice of aircraft and styles of study. Unlike the integrated course, which is full-time and highly structured to make sure that everything you do is completed at specific times as per the flight training school's approved syllabus, the 200-hour syllabus is much more flexible, meaning you can take a little more ownership of what you choose to do at certain phases of the training. You have lessons at your own pace to fit your life outside of flying. There are flight schools that do have a 200-hour syllabus course that is offered full-time with similar duration times as the 150-hour course. However, it is the flexible nature of the course that lends itself to being a part-time course.

A bonus of this course is that it does not have to be as fast paced as the integrated course if you don't want it to be. The flight school is there to teach the RPL, the PPL, and then the CPL; however, it's the hours in between that you have more freedom to select. Not all people who complete a CPL start off their flying enrolled in a CPL course. The 200-hour CPL is suited to these people. Sometimes we have people who are fortunate to start flying at a young age. The minimum age requirement for a CPL is 18 years old, but there are many people who start flying as young as 15, which is the minimum age for your first solo. One of my youngest students who started at age 11 is now a CPL and working as a pilot. When students start at such a young age completing a couple of lessons a month, they are not enrolled in an integrated course and likely to have several flying hours by the time they reach their eighteenth birthday. They would be a perfect fit for this 200-hour non-integrated course. Completing the CPL flight test on their eighteenth birthday is a pretty impressive feat.

It's not only younger pilots who can take advantage of the 200-hour CPL syllabus. It could be private pilots who have been flying for many years decide to upgrade their licence to the CPL for a career change. Often it is people who have full-time jobs and only fly on their days off and holidays. There are many life scenarios the 200-hour syllabus benefits.

How long does a 200-hour CPL take?

Unlike the full-time 150-hour integrated CPL there is no scheduled time to complete the 200-hour course. It is up to the individual in discussion with the flight training school to set out a schedule of training. By sheer math, 200 hours is longer than 150 hours, however it may not always take longer. As an individual you could speed up the process as the course is pitched at your availability and learning pace, not the schedule of the group class set by the flight school. As a 200-hour CPL student you are training at your own pace with the assistance and guidance from the flight school. The average time for a 150-hour integrated CPL course is between 11 to 18 months full-time. It is quite possible to complete the 200-hour course part-time over the same time frame. This does require some planning by the student and discipline to stick to your schedule. Becoming a pilot is a disciplined profession and you should treat this planning phase as one of the first disciplined steps towards achieving your goal.

AN EXAMPLE OF HOW THE 200-HOUR CPL MAY WORK FOR YOU

James started flying part-time whilst at school saving up for his lessons with his part-time job. He is now finished school and wants to complete the course whilst he works full-time. What he does next is up to him, the flying hours he has already obtained still count towards his licence, so he continues from where he left off. He has already completed a theory course for his RPL which he did during his school holidays, and he then schedules his flight lessons to finish the remainder of the RPL syllabus and obtains his RPL after the flight test.

Now he has an RPL he takes some of his school mates flying while he studies for his PPL theory which includes navigation, meteorology, air law and human performance. His hard work pays off and he passes the exam and starts his navigation training. The navigation part of the training is approximately eight or nine cross country navigation exercises with two being solo. James schedules these with his flight school at one per weekend so he has time to prepare and starts on his CPL theory subjects two evenings a week.

At the time of obtaining his PPL, James has passed three of the seven CPL examinations and continues to study for the remaining 4 CPL subjects. Whilst he is studying the remainder of the CPL subjects he plans an interstate flying trip that he will take during his three weeks annual leave. This trip is planned to take at least 40 hours of flying and he is sharing the cost of the flying with his older brother and best mate. James and his brother had always wanted to see the outback of Australia and fly around Uluru since they were children, and this was a perfect opportunity for them to finally experience this.

Whilst flying around Australia, James was checking out some future employers. Each airport he landed at, he took the time to see what type of flying operations were there. Even when he was refueling his aeroplane, he was making connections and meeting people that may be looking for a pilot in the future. On his travels, James had the opportunity to ask different air charter operators questions about their aircraft fleet and if they had any prerequisites for the pilots they employ.

A trip like this is a great way to see the country and and the employment options for pilots; this may help the direction you want to take after the CPL. Australia is a big country and the aviation industry is fairly small.

After completion of this trip James had one more CPL subject exam to study which was Air Law, he had completed the course before the trip but didn't have time to sit the exam until he returned. The Air Law exam is an open book exam, and he was confident after completing some practice exams he could find the required answers in the official documents. Once this exam was completed James decided he wanted to learn to fly at night so completed his Night VFR Rating (more on this will be covered in chapter 6) and continued to spend his weekends going away and building his flying hours.

Once James was within 10 hours of his 100 hours command time, he arranged with his flight instructor to start his commercial pilot training. The first step was learning to fly an aircraft with a propeller that has an adjustable pitch. This involved a few hours training and the aircraft a little bit faster than what he was used to, so things happened more quickly. After mastering how to fly the larger, quicker aircraft, he then had to learn how to navigate at a faster speed and to tighter tolerances. The CPL training course was 20 hours and it was like completing the RPL and PPL together in a faster more complex aircraft.

James was a disciplined pilot and while completing his command time, he always flight planned as he had been taught. James ensured he flew like his instructor was there watching him and he didn't get tempted to cut any corners or just get lazy. This discipline served him well, as he performed well in his CPL training and passed his flight test on the first attempt.

Now James had a plan to obtain a CPL and still worked full-time whilst he did this. His original plan did not include having a night rating. However, it was after his big trip to the outback he thought that flying at night could have been advantageous to his trip, so he wasn't as restricted to landing 10 minutes before last light. With the 200-hour CPL the ability to change the plan along the way is not difficult and up to the individual.

James paid for all his flying as he went, so each time he flew for an hour or more he paid the amount owing at the end of his flight. He also paid for the part-time evening theory courses as he required them. The CPL component of his flying was a birthday present from his family. He forfeited the car.

An advantage of this non-integrated course is that there are no time pressures associated with the training. There is flexibility to adjust the course to suit your schedule and needs. You are in the pilot seat and can make the decisions as to which way you want to proceed, where you want to proceed and what type of aircraft you want to proceed in.

Like James, this course allows you to have control over the different components of the course. You can book flights around your schedule and take theory courses when they suit you. You even have the option of not taking a theory course and selecting to self-study the theory at your own leisure. One of the most enjoyable parts of the 200-hour CPL course is the hours building. You can plan where you would like to fly across the country, and Australia is a great country for flying around. When you speak to career pilots, the flying time they will reflect upon most fondly is those command hours when they were building time towards their CPL.

James shared the cost of some of his flights with his friends. In particular the large outback flight of 40 hours was split between him, his brother and best

The Long and the Short of it - the 200-hour Commercial Pilot Licence (CPL)

> mate amounting to just under 14 hours each which was a considerable saving. As a private pilot, you are permitted to share the cost of an aeroplane up to six seats equally with those onboard. This "cost share" process can reduce the expenses of gaining hours considerably and having family and friends share in your passion is highly rewarding. Imagine a trip to Broome, Kakadu, Cairns or across the Nullarbor, seeing places you would never dream of driving to. Pilots gaining their command time for their CPL often find the location of their first flying job whilst hour building.

Flexibility in the 100-hour Command Time

As you have already seen the 200-hour CPL has a lot of flexibility to be molded into a course to suit the individual.

The 100-hour command time may be 30 hours more than in the 150-hour integrated course (remember 70 command hours minimum) however the 100 hours are not specifically on routes selected by the flight school or in aircraft as determined by the flight training course. If you wanted to gain a multi-engine class rating (chapter 6) you could then spend some of those hours in command flying a multi-engine aircraft. Similar to James, if you wished to obtain a night VFR rating you could have gained some of those hours at night. Another advantage is that you could also be travelling or based in another state for a while and hire an aircraft to take flying from a different flight school, and these hours will all count towards your 200-hours experience. There is one specific requirement in the CPL command time that the pilot conducts a 300-nautical mile flight with two landings which does not include the departure aerodrome. James' outback flight met this requirement.

It is possible you may be fortunate to have a friend who owns an aeroplane and they let you hire it from them, this flying time also counts providing you appropriately log it in your pilot log book.

You don't have to buy a plane?

We have been talking about hour building and the various ways in which you can do this. There is a bit of a misconception that, "If I get a pilot licence, I'm now going to have to buy an aeroplane." Just as you get a driver's licence, you buy a car. You get a motorbike licence, you buy a motorbike. Although many second hand aeroplanes are cheaper than a new car, it is not common to purchase an aeroplane when you have a pilot licence. More often pilots will hire an aeroplane from a flight training school.

If you did want to purchase an aircraft most flight schools can train you in your own aircraft. Aircraft ownership is another area where you need to do your homework. For the training side of things, it would be wise to discuss this with the flight school to see how to proceed with this prior to purchasing the aircraft. A call to the accountant to discuss the merits of aircraft ownership would also be a good idea.

Another method of aircraft hire is becoming part of a syndicate where you may own a share of an aeroplane with several others and have specific usage times and reduced hire rates. However, it is not just the hire of the aircraft you pay for, you are also responsible for a share of the aircraft's maintenance. Like learning to fly and doing your research early, purchasing or hiring an aircraft needs homework too.

Theory Training

The theory syllabus for the CPL is the same regardless of the integrated or non-integrated course. James completed his theory training for all his subjects by attending classes held at the flying school. Most flying

The Long and the Short of it – the 200-hour Commercial Pilot Licence (CPL)

schools conduct theory classes, these may be part-time or full-time. There are also theory schools you can attend and learn the theory subjects only or you may select an online course of study. The option of self-study is also permitted in the 200-hour CPL course. All these options are available to you. You can mix and match the methods of study to suit. You may pick the subjects you find easy to self-study and book into a course for the ones that are more complex. You can even hire your instructor to tutor you in some of the concepts you are finding difficult. There are plenty of practice exams available to complete before you commit to taking the examination.

Regardless of which method of study you select the CASA exams will be conducted online. The RPL and PPL theory may be completed at a flight school. The seven CPL subjects must be completed at a CASA examination centre run by ASPEQ Assessment specialists.

If you are self-studying for these exams, it is important to set yourself a time schedule as the time from the first examination to the last examination must not exceed two years. If for example, you went two years and two months when you took your last exam, you would not be able to include the first exam, only the ones inside that two year period, so you would need to retake the expired exam. Once you have the complete set of exams passed, this will then be permanently valid.

Understanding how the system works and planning your own schedule is one of the advantages of the 200-hour CPL. It may feel a little overwhelming at this stage as there has been a lot of information to take in. It's okay to feel that way, you have done so well to get to this point in the book. Like I mentioned at the beginning, there is quite a lot to know about getting a CPL. Take a breath, and then another, then keep reading as it will become easier as you start to absorb the information. When you finally do make your plan your flight instructor should be able to take a look at it and answer your questions and provide suggestions.

The Left Seat

The most common order of the seven CPL exams is as follows:

Subject	Exam duration	Pass percentage
Meteorology	1.5 hours	70
Human Performance	1.25 hours	70
Navigation	1.75 hours	70
Aerodynamics	1.5 hours	70
Aircraft General Knowledge	1.5 hours	70
Operation Performance & Flight Planning	2.5 hours	70
Flight Rules & Air law	2.0 hours	80

In James' story it mentioned the 200-hour CPL course component being similar to the flying you did in your RPL and PPL only in a faster aircraft and to a higher standard. Part of the training is dedicated to general flying of the higher performance aircraft and the other part is completing navigation exercises that are designed to mimic a commercial passenger carrying flight. Prior to your flight test, your instructor will ensure both your flying and theory knowledge are competent. You will have received a Knowledge Deficiency Report (KDR) for your seven exam subjects unless you passed with 100%. The KDR will outline the areas where you answered the questions incorrectly. For example, if you scored 85% on your examination, there will be 15% of question topics you needed to do further study on. An approved instructor will go through these areas with you to see that you now have the required knowledge.

The CPL flight test format is like the PPL flight test. First there are questions from the examiner and then a simulated charter scenario you must flight plan. The examiner will act as your charter passenger for the flight. Unlike the PPL, the test route is not given to you until the day of the test, so you need to be proficient at ruling up your maps and completing the details on your flight plan form. The flight component is longer than the PPL but will consist of navigation and general handling of the aircraft. On successful completion of the CPL test you will be issued with the licence from CASA. Just like with the RPL and PPL you cannot use the licence until you have received it in your hand.

The Long and the Short of it - the 200-hour Commercial Pilot Licence (CPL)

The 200-hour CPL is definitely more flexible, and it lends itself to a little more fun along the way, because you're able to plan things that you wish to do.

Learning to fly part-time, depending on how you plan it out, also means that your outlay is being projected over a longer period of time, taking into account the two-year theory expiry. With a longer period of time, it means that you have the ability to be paying it off as you go just as James did without having a large debt at the time you finish your training.

Many people work full-time and are flying part-time. Learning to fly this way may appear harder but it doesn't matter which way you learn you have to work hard. In my experience, people flying part-time appreciate their time limitations and are more focused in the time they have at the flight school. I think this is because to get what they need completed they must ensure they are prepared to make the most of their lessons. Often when you have more time to do something, it gets put off to the next day or the next, which can happen with full-time studies. Part-time studies also give the student a break in between classes to reflect on their studies and absorb what they have learnt - remember back to my fire hose analogy.

The 200-hour CPL is flexible whether it be completed full-time or part-time. The time it takes to complete the training is up to the person taking the course. The aircraft they select for their training is also a personalised decision. There are several different options for theory and once again it is the student's choice. The command time flights have few limitations and can be flown all over the country. The payment of the course is when the expenses are incurred and with the option of stretching the time over a longer period means that that payments are easier to make.

It took me three years of hard work, working full-time and flying part-time to complete my CPL and then a flight instructor rating. I

The Left Seat

left my full-time job to work as a flight instructor. One thing I hugely appreciated was the fact that I did not have any debt at the end of my training. This is often not the case and is something you should consider when you are making your decisions in the planning stages of how you will achieve your licence.

CHAPTER 5

AEROPLANE SPOTTING – AEROPLANE TYPES

If you are an aeroplane spotter or enthusiast, you can probably skip this chapter, particularly if you specialise in small aeroplanes. For this chapter, we are going to cover some of my observations from over 27 years of instructing in light aircraft. This chapter is not just one aircraft against the other, although we will go through some of the different types. It's about what's suitable for you and your training, and about understanding the different purposes for each of the aeroplanes. All this forms part of your research in gaining a pilot's licence. Whether speaking to the flight school, or scanning the internet, you will be armed with the right terminologies.

Over many years of speaking to people about being a pilot, one of the most common questions is, "What type of aeroplane do I learn to fly in?" If I asked a room full of non-pilots the question of, "What aeroplane do you expect to learn to fly in? The most common response would be, "Cessna." To provide a touch of history, the Cessna Aircraft Company

The Left Seat

was established in the late 1920s in Kansas in the USA. They produced aircraft for training as well as larger multi-engine commuter types. So, Cessna is a correct answer to my question but it's not the only answer.

Let's talk about what type of Cessna we train in. The most produced Cessna was the Cessna 172, pronounced "Cessna 1-7-2". This is a four-seat, high-wing training aeroplane.

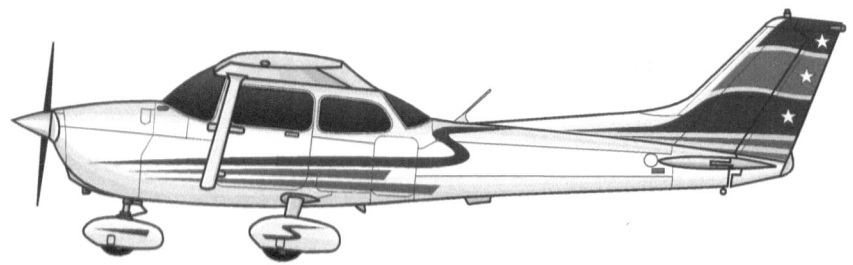

Cessna 172

The Cessna 172 is a popular model with over 43,000 having been produced. If you want to research further, you will find the model or series number usually indicated by a letter, for instance the C172-N or C172-S, among others.

The Cessna aircraft company and others stopped producing aeroplanes in the mid-1980s when litigation and product liability was at a peak. This meant that there were no new Cessna aircraft produced for over 10 years. Then, in the late 1990s, Cessna started producing the C172 again. Many of the world's pilots, both young and old, would have started their training in a Cessna 172.

The beauty of learning to fly and getting a pilot's licence means that you can go from A to B in a straight line. How fast do you do that? Well, when we talk about speed in aeroplanes, we generally talk about it in knots, as in the nautical term. The cruise speed of a Cessna 172 is around 110 knots. When we talk about distance, we talk about nautical

Aeroplane Spotting - Aeroplane Types

miles. 110 knots per hour means the aircraft will fly, in zero wind, a distance of 110 nautical miles in an hour. If you want to equate that to kilometers it is just under 204 km.

Another of the Cessna varieties is the Cessna 152. It is a smaller version of the Cessna 172 with high wing and only 2 seats. Its cruising speed is slightly slower. I read a very apt description of it in an AOPA (I refer to the "Aircraft Owners and Pilots Association" article by Marc Cook who described it as "just sharp enough to teach important lessons but docile enough to protect new students." I've trained many pilots in this aeroplane and would whole-heartedly agree with his summation. An advantage of the C152 is it's smaller and uses less fuel, and therefore more economical to operate, more hours in this size aeroplane when you are learning can reduce the cost of your training.

Around the same time when Cessna was starting to manufacture aeroplanes, there was another manufacturer who started to manufacture the Piper Cherokee. A later version was called the Piper Warrior. This aircraft became a direct competitor to the Cessna 172. It has similar speed characteristics, four seats, and the noticeable difference is, the wings are on the bottom, and it only has one door to enter and exit.

Piper Warrior- PA28

I'm not going to explain all the differences, only the basics, there's plenty more information online if you want to see all the characteristics. I have had people say to me, "I think it looks like a real aeroplane because the wings are on the bottom." Conversely, other people say, "I think aeroplanes look like real aeroplanes when the wings are on the top." Who knows? There is no right or wrong answer, it is all opinion.

In one of the more recent training planes, and I say recent as the Piper and Cessna have been in manufacture for many decades, is the Diamond DA40, which was produced at the turn of the century. The aircraft is a composite construction, not aluminum, with the design look coming from a glider. The DA40 is a four-seat version, and they also have a two-seat version. I have only briefly mentioned these three aircraft, there are several others. If you aren't sure what aeroplanes you're going to be training in, then you need to ask the flight school, so you can do your homework and compare.

There are other types of aircraft that operate in the Recreational Aviation Australia space. RAAus was briefly touched on earlier and is the body with whom these aircraft are registered. A basic look at how you can tell an RAAus aircraft from a non-RAAus aircraft. RAAus aircraft will have a series of 6 numbers on the rear of the aircraft. In Australia, all aircraft that are registered with CASA have VH at the front, and then be followed by three letters.

VH registered aircraft are registered by the Civil Aviation Safety Authority, and numbers aeroplane are registered by RAAus. An RAAus aircraft, has one or two seats, so is quite small in comparison to many VH registered aircraft. However, just because they're small doesn't mean they can't be fast and fitted out with all the latest technology.

Some of the common RAAus aircraft used in training are a Tecnam, a Jabiru, a Foxbat, and a Sling. These aircraft, because of their weight categories, can actually be registered under the VH registration, or the RAAus registration. Under the current aviation regulations in the light aircraft, or very light aircraft categories, you can have the same type of aeroplane with different types of registration. This can be a bit confusing to new entrants into the industry.

RAAus is an active part of the general aviation community with new aircraft being added to its ranks regularly. Many years ago, it was considered for the home-built type aeroplanes which were lightweight and reasonably basic. But over time, these aeroplanes have developed into some very sophisticated machines with lots of new and innovative equipment on board. Demand grows innovation. In this section of the industry there is quite the demand.

We'll take the Tecnam, the same aeroplane, but in different registrations. What does this mean?

A Tecnam registered with RAAus may be restricted to the air space it can fly, independent on the licence of the pilot. The maintenance of the aircraft is not required to be signed off by a Licensed Aircraft Maintenance Engineer (LAME). The pilot who flies this aircraft must be a member of RAAus and have an RAAus pilot certificate. A Tecnam registered in VH registration is not restricted to the type of air space it can fly in. The maintenance of the aircraft is required to be signed off by a LAME, and the person flying it holds a licence issued by the Civil Aviation Safety Authority. There are several instances of pilots having both CASA and RAAus qualifications and being able to fly in either aircraft.

Should I fly in a high-wing or low-wing aeroplane as I always thought that low-wings look like real aeroplanes?

The training syllabus is the same for both the high-wing, and the low-wing aeroplanes. From experience watching students training in both, I've noticed that when a student transitions from one type to the other, there is one transition that appears easier. A student who has flown in a high-wing aeroplane and transfers to a low-wing aeroplane, appears to pick up the skill-set quicker. It often seems to take longer for a student who flies in a low-wing aeroplane to become competent in flying the high-wing.

Two Engines

A more complex model is a multi-engine aeroplane which, as the name suggests, is an aeroplane with more than one engine, sometimes referred to as a twin-engine aeroplane. Pilots need to have a minimum of a PPL before they can undertake a course of training to gain a Multi-Engine Aeroplane class rating (MEA). That training may vary depending on the complexity of the aircraft and the previous experience of the pilot. It could be anywhere between five to ten hours. With two engines comes greater expense. The complexity of a MEA may demand more regular flying to remain at a level of competence to handle the emergency procedures when one engine fails.

You are unlikely to ever meet a pilot who doesn't aspire to fly an additional aeroplane with additional, more complex features. This desire is common amongst pilots regardless of experience. There is always something you'd like to add to your skill set.

I know a retired airline pilot with many thousands of hours who said he always wanted to fly a Cessna 210. This is a six-seat high-wing aeroplane. He'd flown different aeroplanes all over the world, but this particular aeroplane was not listed in his logbook to date.

Glass Cockpit Aircraft

When I started flying, the term glass cockpit wasn't used when someone was explaining to you about learning to fly. But then again, the flying school had a phone with a dial, a mobile phone came in a bag that looked somewhat like a large camera bag and a computer had a green screen. Technology has changed how we do things.

Aeroplane Spotting - Aeroplane Types

When you hear a person mention the aeroplane has a glass cockpit what does this mean?

Earlier in this chapter, I mentioned Cessna 172 aeroplanes being built 40 plus years ago. The flight instruments, such as the airspeed indicator which tells the pilot how fast the aircraft is flying or the altimeter that tells the pilot how high the aircraft is, are what we refer to as analogue instruments or round dials. Think back to some of the WWII two aeroplane movies where the pilot is seated with a whole panel of round dial instruments in front of them. The glass cockpit is more like a computer screen in front of the pilot with the same instruments as before but now represented in a digital format. Instead of a dial-like airspeed indicator with a needle pointing to the speed similar to what you see in many cars, there is a speed tape which indicates the speed. The C172 aeroplane flies the same as it used to, and the aerodynamics of the aeroplane are the same. The change is in how the upgraded instruments display information.

Modern passenger airliners are all fitted with glass cockpits. There are varied opinions on whether learning to fly in glass aircraft is beneficial to the future airline pilot. There are plenty of airline pilots who have flown both analogue and glass cockpits. I've watched pilots transition from glass cockpit instruments to analog instruments and vice versa. It is the skill of adaptability which is needed in either case.

After a pilot obtains their CPL they will often go and fly some of the larger Cessna and Piper commuter type aircraft. Many of these aircraft in the general aviation sector are still analogue, because they were built at the same time as the original Cessna 172 and Piper Warriors. Some of these aircraft may have been retrofitted with glass instruments however a large percentage of the aeroplanes in Australia, between training and the airliners, are likely to have analogue instruments.

Aircraft Design Features

Aircraft design features are additional features the aircraft may have which will require the pilot to be specifically trained on because there is an additional degree of skill and knowledge required to operate the aircraft.

Manual Pitch Propeller Control
The C172 and the PA28 both have fixed pitch propellers, meaning the blade angle of the propeller does not change. A manual pitch propeller is where the pilot can change the blade angle of the propeller to make it more efficient in different phases of flight. If a pilot is training for their CPL, this design feature is one of the requirements for the CPL flight test. Some examples of common aircraft used are the Cessna 182, Piper Arrow, Diamond Star and Tobago.

Retractable undercarriage is another common design feature which is self-explanatory, meaning that the pilot can put the wheels up and down. Most people find this quite an easy function to learn, however, as obvious as it may seem, I am sure you have probably heard of instances or seen news reports where the wheels have not extended, or the pilot has forgotten to extend them prior to landing.

Tail Wheel Design Feature
Most training aeroplanes don't have a tail wheel. Instead, they have a tricycle undercarriage. There are still several aeroplanes that have a tailwheel and if you speak to a tail wheel endorsed pilot, they will tell you of the unique take-off and landing techniques required to keep the aeroplane straight on the runway.

Float Plane
This is where the aircraft is fitted with floats so it can land on water instead of a hard surface. In Australia there are not huge volumes of these aircraft. Whereas if we were in Canada, both float plane and ski landing gear to land on snow would be more popular.

Aeroplane Spotting – Aeroplane Types

Let me tell you a story about George. George had always wanted to get a pilot's licence, and it was in his mid-twenties, he had the time and means to learn to fly. He started off flying in the Cessna 152 because this was the most economical of the aeroplanes, and he didn't see any point in spending money to fly something with more than two seats in the initial parts of his training. When learning to fly the aeroplane back and forth to the local training area, there was no need for anyone to be in the back. After he completed the first stage of his licence, he spent a few months flying friends out to the training area while he studied for his PPL. He was comfortable in the Cessna152, but he wanted to challenge himself, and he wanted to take more friends flying. He arranged to be checked out, with an instructor, in the Cessna 172 because it was a bit faster, a bit heavier, and easier to handle than the C152. Overall, the flying skills he needed were still the same.

George completed his PPL in the Cessna 172. After a few months with his PPL and a few weekend trips away with friends, he was looking for another challenge and asked if he could fly the PA-28 Piper Warrior. Now, his licence allowed him to fly this aeroplane, technically. However, there is a general competency rule which means you need to be competent in an aircraft prior to flying it. To meet this requirement, he first studied the aircraft handbook and completed the PA28 engineering paper. To ensure that he was competent at flying, he completed a dual flight with an instructor, covering the general handling techniques of the aircraft, and some take-offs and landings and practice emergency procedures. He reported flying the low-wing was actually easier in the crosswind landings than he'd found in the Cessna 172. For the next 18 months, George flew over 50 hours and had been as far as Adelaide, Sydney, and some parts of Central New South Wales.

George had held his PPL for two years and it was time for George's flight review. A flight review is a procedure that a pilot must do with an approved instructor every two years to revalidate their licence. He was keen to make a trip to Brisbane but would like an aeroplane a little bit faster. Following a discussion with his instructor, he decided to upgrade his skills and learn to fly a new aircraft type the Piper Arrow. The Piper Arrow has a propeller that can change pitch and a retractable under carriage. He completed the manual pitch propeller control and retractable undercarriage design features training. After this additional training, his licence was revalidated and was good to go for another two years. George was able to fly his partner up to Brisbane, where they stayed for a week before flying home.

When you're carrying passengers, you need to ensure that you have performed three take-offs and landings in the last 90 days. If he doesn't have a trip planned or if it's winter and he's not feeling like flying too far, George makes sure that he comes in and flies those three takeoffs and landings every 90 days to keep himself current. George's story is just one of the ways in which you can use your licence and change from one aircraft to another. George is now looking at upgrading his skills and including a multi-engine class rating. George is still a private pilot and enjoys his flying.

Aeroplane Spotting - Aeroplane Types

No matter what aircraft you choose to complete your pilot licence training, the important thing is that you do your research to make sure you understand the aircraft type you will be training in. This will assist you in knowing what somebody is talking about when you start asking questions about your future training. Good luck, and if you have any questions, always ask your flight instructor. Instructors love to have students that ask questions rather than take things for granted. Your curious nature will put you in good stead to becoming a good pilot.

CHAPTER 6

KNOW WHAT YOU ARE LOOKING FOR – RATINGS AND ENDORSEMENTS

By this stage of the book, you may have an idea about which type of pilot licence you want to obtain, either a PPL or a CPL. This chapter is going to talk about the different ratings and upskills that you can complete and add on to your licence. It's important to have a look at how and in which order you want to complete these, as people can be easily sold into training courses they don't need due to a lack of knowledge. The flying school may channel you into a pathway they desire which matches the courses they offer and not necessarily the pathway that you wished. The whole purpose of this book is to give you an overview of the different offerings so that you can understand and know more about pilot training. This will enable you to complete further research, so you can make your own informed decisions.

The Left Seat

One of the add-ons you can make to your pilot licence is what is commonly referred to by pilots as the CSU or constant speed unit. So as not to confuse, this is technically called the Manual Pitch Propeller Control (MPPC) design feature. What is a CSU/MPPC? I could put my instructor hat on and go into detail, however at this point you are likely to glaze over. Remember George in the previous chapter when he decided he wanted to take a faster aircraft the Piper Arrow (PA28R) to Brisbane, this was one of the design features he needed. In basic terms, the aircraft has the ability to change the angle of the blade on the propeller by the pilot moving a control inside the cockpit, making the aircraft more efficient when it is flying and hence faster.

In Australia, if you are completing a CPL you will need to have this design feature endorsement. This is because the CPL flight test must be performed in an aircraft with this feature and the speed of the aircraft must be a minimum of 120 kts. Unlike in some other countries, you cannot complete a CPL in a Cessna 152, Cessna 172 or Piper Warrior (PA28) as these aircraft do not have a manual pitch propeller.

The MPPC is one common design feature, another is retractable undercarriage (RUC). This design feature is self-explanatory, the wheels on the aeroplane go up (retract) and the wheels on the aeroplane go down. The pilot can control this feature and must be trained in the correct operation. It may appear obvious as to when the wheels go up, such as after take-off, and down prior to landing, however it is important the pilot has strict checking routines to ensure this does occur. A common saying regarding retractable undercarriages is, "There are two types of pilots those who have had a wheels up landing and those that will." I am currently in the latter and hope to keep it that way for my career. Many aircraft, including the Piper Arrow that George was flying, have both the MPPC and RUC so the design feature training on both would be completed at the same time.

Know What You Are Looking For – Ratings and Endorsements

Float Plane Design Feature

Although float planes are less common in Australia, there are companies that offer float plane endorsements. Additional rules of the water will also need to be learned. The training organisation will take you through a course of training and approve you once you have completed and met the required competency standard. As there are not as many float planes compared to conventional land-based aircraft the opportunities to hire the aircraft are limited.

Tail Wheel Design Feature

In the early years of aviation, most aircraft were tail wheel aircraft, however as time progressed so did the design to tricycle undercarriage. The majority of conventional training aircraft are tricycle undercarriage, they have a nose wheel, and two main wheels one either side of the aircraft. A tail wheel aircraft has the two main wheels and a tail wheel. There are still some older aircraft with tail wheels, as well as some new aircraft, often in the aerobatic aircraft range. I won't give a lesson on gyroscopic forces. However, the tail wheel aircraft pilot requires certain skills to control the aircraft, particularly close to the ground on take-off and landing. A tail wheel design feature endorsement is a challenge for any conventional tricycle undercarriage pilot which is why it warrants its own design feature endorsement.

Other design features include a floating hull, centerline thrust, ski landing gear, all of these design features will involve a course of training and once you have achieved competence the relevant paperwork will be completed. The course durations may vary depending on the aircraft and the flight school so be sure to ask when you get to this point. Training for the design feature endorsement must be with an approved instructor, however other than achieving competence in the training there is no separate flight test with an examiner required.

The Left Seat

Before I start to talk about multi-engine aircraft, I want to expand on the centre-line thrust design feature - a centerline thrust aircraft has two engines so technically is a multi-engine but because one engine is mounted on the front of the aircraft, like a single engine aircraft (pulling the aircraft through the air) the other engine is mounted at the rear of the aircraft (pushing the aircraft through the air). A Cessna 337 is an example of this type of aircraft (affectionately referred to as a "suck and blow"). If either of these engines fail, there will be a loss of performance but there will not be any asymmetric control issues and handling the controls would not change.

The Multi-Engine Aeroplane Class Rating (MEA)

The MEA is another upskill a pilot may select to add to their licence. The training for this rating will vary. The initial MEA is a minimum of five hours. However, depending on the previous experience of the pilot and the complexity of the multi-engine aeroplane being flown, the time to reach competency will vary. The twin-engine aeroplane that you complete your MEA on will have a manual pitch propeller control and most often retractable undercarriage. It is possible to complete these design feature endorsements at the same time as you complete the MEA. A multi-engine, sometimes referred to as a twin-engine aeroplane, has an engine on either wing. Much of the training in this rating is teaching the pilot what to do in the event of one engine failing. Unlike the centerline thrust aircraft, if one engine fails the engine still running will want to turn the aeroplane the direction of the failed engine. This situation, if not managed efficiently and correctly, could result in something disastrous happening to the aircraft. This training is completed with a multi-engine approved flight instructor and after the instructor has completed your training you will undertake a separate flight test with a flight examiner before being issued with your MEA.

Is a Multi-Engine Aeroplane Class Rating Mandatory for a CPL?

The Multi-Engine Aeroplane class rating may be included in the CPL syllabus, along with the design feature and manual pitch propeller control, in a bundled package. It is not a mandated requirement, you can always complete a single engine CPL and then obtain a multi-engine class rating after the CPL and that will give you a multi-engine CPL. When you start to look at what you want to do with the CPL, the MEA may increase your ability to be able to gain employment depending on where you are looking to work. Once again you will need to complete your research and check what aircraft and experience requirements your future employer operates and needs, and progress your training to your maximum benefit.

The Aerobatics Flight Activity Endorsement

Many people have been inspired to fly by attending an airshow and looking in wonderment as an aircraft performs loops and rolls and lots of other acrobatic maneouvres across the sky. If there is one rating that really helps you improve your flying skills and make you a more confident and competent pilot it is the aerobatics endorsement. Just learning the basics puts the pilot and aircraft in situations that hopefully you'll never experience and gives you the confidence and ability to recover. If you are already an aviation enthusiast, you will have read about aircraft accidents and pilots losing their hands-on flying skills. Aerobatics is another way to improve these skills and have lots of fun along the way.

The Formation Flight Activity Endorsement

Whether it be at airshows or memorial services, like the Anzac Day parades, you'll see a gaggle of aeroplanes, or formation of aeroplanes flying in a pattern overhead. This type of flying requires a specific skill and it is something that you can add on to your pilot licence. It will involve a course of training and because this training involves more than one aircraft, there may be others training with you at the same time.

Night VFR Rating

In chapter 4, we heard about James's journey to a CPL and on the way he completed a Night VFR Rating. The PPL is under a set of rules called the Visual Flight Rules or VFR. This means that pilots follow a set of rules to enable them to fly by day and not in the clouds. Pilots navigate by reference to a map and seeing visual features on the ground. The Night VFR rating allows the pilot to fly at night; however, the visual rules still apply as the Night VFR pilot cannot fly in cloud and must also be able to navigate with reference to visual cues on the ground. This rating is useful if you want to fly later in the day and extend that trip or early morning before the sun has risen.

A night VFR rating consists of a minimum 10 hours at night including two hours in the circuit pattern learning to take off and land with minimal visual cues and five hours of cross-country navigation. The cross-country navigation is more difficult as you only have lights from towns, traffic or roads to navigate by. It has become easier now as most aircraft are fitted with GPS (Global Positioning System). Most people are familiar with what a GPS is as they are in cars and mobile phones. Twenty years ago, it was rare to find a night VFR aircraft fitted with a GPS.

Navigation in an area that is remote from ground lighting when the ground is black and the overcast night sky even blacker, your reliance on flight instruments becomes more critical. Careful attention also needs to be paid to weather forecasts as you don't want to inadvertently fly into cloud.

Know What You Are Looking For - Ratings and Endorsements

At the completion of the training, there is a flight test with an examiner. If the flight test is completed in a single-engine you can only pilot a single-engine aircraft at night. If the flight test is completed in a multi-engine aircraft, you are permitted to pilot a single or a multi-engine aircraft at night.

The Instrument Rating

If you ask any instrument rated pilot, they are likely to say that the instrument rating was a significant challenge when they first started their training. Depending on which licence you hold when you commence an instrument rating, you will have had minimal exposure to flying on instruments. You have learned the set of rules for visual flying now you must learn another set of rules to apply when instrument flying.

An instrument rating is considered a professional rating and it involves being able to navigate on instruments. The ability to navigate on instruments means you are permitted to fly in the clouds and no longer limited to visual navigation. Now this next sentence may seem a little confusing, but you can be flying under the instrument flight rules on a perfectly blue sky day as it is a set of skills and procedures a pilot uses when they go flying.

Imagine flying amidst cloud, having lost all your visual cues as to where you are located or if the aeroplane is level or turning. The instrument rating teaches you skills to be able to fly the aircraft safely in these conditions. It assists you to navigate the aircraft to the destination and perform a specific instrument procedure to land safely.

When you visit most major airports, you'll see the aircraft coming in one after the other to land. If it is a cloudy day you will often see the lights burst through the cloud when the aircraft is on its final approach lined up with the runway. These aircraft are following a specific instrument procedure they have been trained in to enable them to navigate through the cloud and then to position the aircraft in the correct location with the runway in front of them avoiding any nearby terrain or obstacles.

Gaining this skill takes a considerable amount of time and practice. That is why an instrument rating involves 40 hours of flying on instruments. Some of this instrument time, often 20 hours, is spent in a flight simulator or trainer with the pilot practicing their skill before taking to the real aircraft. If the skies are blue when the pilot is training the flight instructor has a hood or foggles (frosted glasses) they place on the student which limits their vision to inside the cockpit to enable them to experience the availability of outside visual cues.

Just as there was an air law component in the PPL and CPL theory licences there is also a theory examination covering the Instrument Flight Rules (IFR) called IREX. On completion of the instrument rating course there is a flight test with a flight examiner. The duration of the test will vary depending on what type of approaches you have decided to add to the rating. Approaches are the specific procedures a pilot can fly to safely descend the aircraft to arrive at the airport.

When Can You Complete an Instrument Rating?

You must have a minimum of a PPL to undertake an instrument rating. Along with the 40 hours of instrument flying which you complete in the training you also need 50 hours cross country command time. It is wise to have this command time completed prior to the commencement of your instrument training. Many courses include both the CPL and instrument rating because it is part of the pathway towards getting their qualifications to apply to an airline. An airline pilot, which we talk about later, will hold an instrument rating. It is not a requirement to complete the instrument rating straight after finishing the CPL. A pilot may choose to wait until they have more flying experience before they take up this more advanced training. Unlike the two-year validity period of the PPL and CPL the instrument rating requires revalidation of skills every 12 months in the form of an instrument proficiency check with a flight examiner.

It is not only a proficiency check every 12 months that is required to keep currency for the instrument rating. There are additional approach recency requirements, some of which can be completed in a simulator. Flying under the IFR is a perishable skill, so if a pilot is not flying IFR regularly, they will need to complete some additional refresher training prior to undertaking their annual proficiency check. This upkeep of skills can often prove expensive if there was no immediate need to hold the instrument rating. Unfortunately, I have seen several pilots who let the instrument rating lapse because of the expense of keeping it updated so I suggest you think seriously as to whether you will be able to maintain the proficiency before you undertake the training.

The instrument rating can also be completed with the additional academic qualification of the Diploma of Aviation – Instrument rating.

There is another type of instrument rating called the Private IFR. This rating is not able to be used as a professional qualification. There is a similar examination to the IREX, but it doesn't include any of the commercial operations questions. There are 20 required flying hours, and the proficiency check requirements are every two years as a flight review with an approved instructor.

The Flight Instructor Rating

In most cases you require a CPL prior to completing a flight instructor rating. I chose the pathway of flight instructor after achieving my CPL and personally have found teaching others is one of the most rewarding parts of my career. A flight instructor rating will allow you to work for a flight training school and teach people to fly an aeroplane. The

The Left Seat

flight instructor rating is a course of training which includes both flying skills and teaching skills.

There is a theory examination called the flight instructor rating exam which covers various topics on instructing methods and techniques. The duration of flight instructor rating course varies between flight schools from 30-50 hours. The inclusions in these courses will also vary so you need to ensure you are fully aware of what the course contains.

The initial instructor rating generally starts as a grade 3 instructor. After the initial rating, you can add on additional training endorsements. Each training endorsement will have prerequisites, a course of training and test. Instructor ratings are in grades starting at a grade 3, then grade 2, and then the senior grade 1 instructor.

When you become an instructor, you must learn to fly again from the opposite seat. The pilot command seat is the left seat however as an instructor you learn fly from the right seat. I have heard it said it is good preparation to becoming a first officer in an airline as you already can fly from that seat position.

The flight instructor rating is not just about learning to instruct a student in the aircraft. There are many hours spent on the course learning how to present and teach topics from the flying training syllabus. You may have passed the theory exams on all the topics you are teaching, however it is a long-held theory as Richard Feynman says, "If you want to master something teach it".

As the hours of an instructor rating course can vary between flight schools the duration of the course will also vary. On average the flight instructor rating courses that are conducted full-time are anywhere between six to ten weeks. The grade 3 course will include classroom theory briefings, both listening to, and delivering flight lessons. The lesson sequences are similar to those of the RPL and PPL but sitting in the instructors' seat on the right-hand side of the aircraft.

Know What You Are Looking For – Ratings and Endorsements

The Flight instructor rating can also be completed with a Diploma of Aviation-Flight Instructor.

INTRODUCING DAMIEN

Damien is a private pilot and he often used to fly to King Island and Flinders Island, located between Victoria on the mainland and the island of Tasmania. His motivation for travelling to both islands was a love of fishing and crayfish. Damien would often fly to these islands with friends and stay for the weekend. As a private pilot, he had added A Night VFR rating to his licence enabling him to maximise the daylight on the island on the weekends and would arrive back to the mainland about half an hour after last light.

After a couple of years making this trip he added the MPPC and RUC endorsements to his licence so that he could travel that little bit faster and take a larger aircraft with six seats instead of four. He didn't take more passengers instead the extra load capability meant he could carry more baggage which was appreciated in winter when he would stay on the island for up to a week at a time.

When flying to either of these islands Damien would use a procedure commonly called island hopping. This is where he tracked, flying over small land masses to enable him to reach his destination. The reasoning for this was that he was flying in a single-engine aircraft, and, if in the very unlikely event the engine failed, there would be a land mass nearby to either land on or near instead of in the middle of the water. Island hopping is quite a common practice for light aircraft pilots who wish to fly to Tasmania and considered an added safety measure. It also gives them visual cues to navigate by. Pilots also use this form of island hop procedure to fly to New Zealand from Australia via Lord Howe and Norfolk Island.

For Damien, island-hopping was slightly longer than if he flew direct which is one of the bonuses of air travel so Damien decided he would undertake the multi-engine class rating. With the course of training complete and the flight test passed he was now able to fly direct in an even faster aircraft than previously used. The safety of the additional engine was a comfort to his well flown passengers (his family) and, in the unlikely event of an engine failure, the aircraft could still fly with one engine to the destination.

About six months later when it was coming into winter and the days were shorter, Damien added the multi-engine night VFR rating to his flying skills as until then he was only permitted to fly single engine by night. Damien was a regular flyer and had logged several flying hours not only flying to the Islands but across Australia as well. It was one early spring morning when Damien had planned to fly down to Tasmania for a long weekend that the weather turned bad around halfway on his trip and he had to turn around and fly back to his departure point. It was after this experience that Damien made the decision to enrol in an instrument rating course. He was a private pilot, however he decided to take the professional instrument rating theory exam IREX and then undertake the instrument rating training. Damien had over 200 cross country flying hours and more than 60 of these in the multi-engine aircraft so was extremely

Know What You Are Looking For – Ratings and Endorsements

comfortable in the twin-engine aircraft that he was going to train in.

The training consisted of 40 hours instrument flying with 20 of those hours in a ground-based simulator learning to fly with reference to the instruments and how to navigate without looking out the window. The most challenging part was learning how to conduct the different instrument approach procedures so he could manoeuvre the aircraft out of the clouds and then position the aircraft for landing. Damien had a full-time Monday to Friday job so he would only fly on weekends. The instrument training took him about four months part-time to complete. Once he passed his flight test, he was able to fly in clouds if the weather was not blue skies.

Damien held a PPL and was able to add all these endorsements and ratings on to his PPL. Now, I have been asked, can I add a multi-engine class rating to my RPL? The rules are no. However, once you have a PPL the ability to add endorsements and ratings is increased.

After obtaining a PPL, the options of ratings are yours. There is no regulated timeframe or order in which you must complete any of these unless you are on an integrated CPL course that has clearly defined terms regarding when this training is to be taken. Otherwise, it's a personal choice, and you decide just as Damien did when the need arose.

CHAPTER 7

WHEN THERE IS TURBULENCE – BARRIERS

When my business first started, one of the things we would often do was to put an aeroplane inside a shopping center. The thought behind this idea was that most of the time when people saw aeroplanes, they were at a distance, either behind a glass window or fence or high up in the sky. Putting an aeroplane in a shopping centre would be a good opportunity for people to see an aeroplane up close where they could touch and feel it. It was amazing how many emotions this simple act triggered for the passers-by. Former WW2 pilots, current pilots, people who knew a pilot, or those who had thought about flying. Everyone had a story to tell, whether from the past or a dream of the future.

I have stood in a shopping centre next to an aeroplane countless times and every time people will come up to me and say, "Gee, I always wanted to fly an aeroplane." That begs the question: if you always wanted to fly an aeroplane, why haven't you done so yet? In this chapter, I will cover some of the reasons or excuses people give that holds them back from their dream to fly.

One of the main reasons is psychological, the mental barrier that prevents us from going ahead and achieving our goal. We may have every intention of doing something, but something holds us back, which often is our own mind. You are one step closer to defeating this by reading this chapter - keep going.

Let's consider some of the more common reasons as to why people haven't started flying.

Many of the pilots I have trained who have established careers outside of aviation have expressed to me that they wished they had started earlier. Their reasons for not starting earlier are usually similar, university, working on their career, marriage, mortgage, and children. If this sounds like you, then you are not alone, however remember their words "they wished they had started earlier." The only time we have for making choices is now, and learning to fly could be one of them. These reasons can often be categorised into money and time - when you are busy earning money, you don't have time to spend it, and when they do have the time they don't necessarily have the funds.

In today's world, it is commonplace for us to say we are always busy. If a person is asked, "How are you?" the response is often, "I've been busy." It's almost if you say you're not busy, there's something wrong with you. Have you ever heard the saying, "If you want something done, give it to a busy person?" If you really want to fly, you will work out a way in which you can do it busy or not. Over the years several of my part-time students have been some of the busiest people I know and loved every minute of their flying training.

Flying involves dedication. Dedication and good time management will allow you to be able to make that time to become a pilot. If there is one constant in this world, it's that everyone is given 24 hours in a day. It is up to you to use this to your advantage. If learning to fly is something you want to do, you need to make the time. Just like you make time for a sport, hobby, going to the gym or doing something with your family, you make the time. Don't let busy be your excuse.

Is time really the excuse? Or is it an easy default excuse? Is there another reason?

Another response I often hear is, " I'm not smart enough. I didn't do math at school." There seems to be this misconception that pilots must be fantastic at math and physics. The general consensus that pilots must be good in these subjects creates an air of "smart" attached to this assumption so why would any pilot debunk the myth? Sure, when I was at school, I studied year 12 math and physics and enjoyed them. One of the reasons why I studied those subjects was because when I used to read through career books, they stated that pilots needed to have completed math and physics.

Studying math and physics won't hinder a pilot, however I've taught many pilots that haven't studied math and physics at school who have had no trouble in understanding the concepts taught. Remember, the theory courses that you need to study when you learn to fly are designed to teach you from scratch, by assuming you know nothing about flying to start with. We're not designing, building or sending the aeroplane to the moon. We are simply flying it. Thinking back to the early aviators, the aeroplanes were fairly basic, and the rules of aerodynamics haven't changed since those early days of aviation.

When I listen to a person who says, "I'm not smart enough," I say to them, "Can you use a calculator? Can you add up? Do you have the ability to learn and the willingness to learn?" If they come back with "yes," and if it is something they are interested in learning, I believe they are capable of passing the required examinations. I've watched many people with these initial thoughts achieve their dream of becoming a pilot.

Please don't let that feeling of you're not smart enough prevent you from taking that first step. Every new beginning is hard, and everything that is new is usually difficult. But it's only difficult until we learn it, and that's the way we need to tackle our mindset right from the beginning when learning to fly. There may be a small percentage of the population who desire to fly and lack the academics to be able pass the required subjects but that would be very small. If academics are your concern, speak with the flying school and find out more about what the study requirements are. You may not have been a high achiever at school. I have taught several pilots who would quite readily say they didn't achieve high marks at secondary school and have still gone on to gain a pilot licence and exceled at their pilot studies. You have heard some of the stories throughout this book of what people really enjoy about flying, and it has to be one of the most amazing things that you could do.

Medical Fitness – Will I Pass?

A common concern of prospective pilots is whether they would pass the aviation medical requirements. As I am not doctor, I am not qualified to go into the specific requirements, which you can discuss with a Designated Aviation Medical Examiner (DAME). There are also further details available on the www.casa.gov.au website.

Aviation medicals are divided into classes. For the CPL, a pilot requires a Class 1 medical and for a PPL, a pilot requires a Class 2. There is also a Basic Class 2 medical that has limitations on passenger numbers and types of operations.

Class 1 involves the following components: the examination by the DAME, hearing test, ECG, blood tests and an ophthalmologist eye test.

If I had a dollar for every time I was told that you need perfect eyesight to be a pilot, I'd be travelling first class on all my holidays. This is a common misconception. For a pilot in the military it is important, however in civilian aviation, corrected vision is accepted. It would be wonderful if we all had 20/20 vision, or the vision of the man who broke the sound barrier Chuck Yeager at 20/7. Once again discuss any concerns with the DAME.

The Class 2 medical can be completed solely by the DAME without the additional tests.

Is It All Over If You Can Only Obtain a Class 2 Medical?

At this point in time, you must hold a Class 1 medical to obtain a CPL. If you can't hold a Class 1 medical commercial flying may not be possible. That does not mean you cannot fly for a living. It is still possible to have a flying career in RAAus as a flying instructor on a Class 2 medical.

How Can I Afford the Course?

Since you started reading this book, you will know it is no secret that flying is expensive. The cost of operating an aeroplane is not cheap, nor would you want it to be. Aircraft need to be serviced regularly by a LAME. The cost of fuel, insurance, landing fees, parking charges, hangarage and the capable flight instructor sitting beside you or supervising your solo flight all add up.

When I learnt to fly, the era of free government-sponsored university degrees was coming to an end, and there was no form of government loan to assist with flying training study. In 2020, the government has VET Student Loans loans for some pilot training courses. A budding student pilot can enrol in a flight training organisation that is approved under the VSL scheme and if they meet the qualifying requirements, they will be granted a student loan to assist with their flying course costs. Like any government study loan, whether it be for a university degree or CPL, it is a loan which eventually you will have to pay back.

One of the penalties of having a student loan, particularly in flying, is that often the courses approved to accept the student loan may appear to be significantly more expensive than those that don't attract the VSL. Ensure you also research on the refund policies, loan interest and repayment schedules and how the loan is allocated to certain blocks of your flying studies. Any course that attracts the VSL will also include the academic diploma component alongside the CASA CPL qualification.

There is often an assumption by students the student loan will cover all your flying costs. This is not always the case and there are likely to be some out-of-pocket expenses. As a student who may not have any regular income, you need to know what those out-of-pocket expenses are to enable you to plan for them, otherwise your course will be interrupted while you source the additional funds to continue.

The majority of flight training schools in Australia do not have the VSLs and, given it is a competitive business market, you are likely to find these courses without government assistance significantly more affordable. The challenge now becomes how you can afford them. I made a comment to a client recently that the course my flight school offers is $20,000 cheaper than the same course offered with a VSL, which is a significant difference. If you decide to take the path of a loan, make sure you understand what is involved.

Browsing through the finance section of the bookstore, there are several books on managing your finances. A popular one that often tops the Google search list is *The Barefoot Investor* by Scott Pape, a book which asks people to put money away for various items. Following these processes has shown in several cases that even the worst of savers can save money with a few disciplined steps.

When There is Turbulence - Barriers

Let's look at disposable income and discretionary spending. I don't drink coffee, and yes I'm often asked what sort of pilot I am as a result, but I watch people come in and out every day, having at minimum two coffees a day. Those two daily coffees add up to $10 a day, five days a week at least. There's $50. In two weeks, there's $100, and so on. Keep track of your discretionary spending and make responsible choices is always sound advice.

It comes down to priorities, which I can't set for you, but I encourage you to set your financial priorities in a way that allows you to achieve your flying goal. If you really want to fly, there are ways in which you can make it happen. Sometimes it might take a little bit longer than you would like. We are living in an era of instant gratification, in which people want to get to their destination as quickly as possible. The need to be in a hurry is part of that mentality of being busy. It is okay to want things now, however learning to fly is not an instant process. Take the time to slow down for a moment and reflect on your priorities.

If learning to fly is low priority for you, then the hard fact is that you won't make it happen. You need to ask yourself is this something you really want to do, and if the answer is yes, you then need to take action towards this. You can read books like this, which are a good start, but you need to make a plan and set a date to start. There is an old saying that "the best time to start was yesterday, the next best time is now." You can take that next step today.

Over the many years during which I have taught students, there have been numerous students who have had more than one job to be able to financially support their flying. These students are usually the ones an instructor finds the most rewarding to teach. They are dedicated, work hard and appreciate every single hour of flying they undertake. They know how hard they worked for the opportunity and don't waste a minute of it. On the flip side, I have sadly seen students who were highly fortunate by not paying for the flying training out of their own pockets. Some of these students lacked preparation for lessons and didn't complete their homework, resulting in the repeat of lessons. As one instructor crudely put it, when you are throwing five dollar notes out the window every minute, you want to make sure you do your homework. The denomination of the notes only increases as the size of the aircraft grows. It shouldn't really matter who is paying for the lesson. To make the most of any of the lessons you need to put in the required effort.

When I was looking at learning to fly, I thought I did my homework. I would scan the yellow pages, call up flight schools, ask questions and get them to send me the information on their courses. I started doing this from about the age of 13. In all my research, the only thing I could see was the huge dollar figure on the bottom line. Where was I ever going to get all that money from? The missing information no one bothered to tell me until I actually started learning to fly was that I didn't need the entire course amount before I even stepped into an aeroplane.

If you are studying for a PPL or the more flexible 200-hour CPL there are options to pay for the flights as you take them. You can also pay for the theory courses and exams as you sit for them. There is no requirement to have the entire amount of the course before you start. I delayed starting to learn to fly due to the misconception that I needed all the money on day one. I thought I had done my homework, I knew how much it cost, how many hours I needed for the licence, but forgot to ask the payment terms. Understanding the payment terms will allow you to plan a budget and determine how long it may take to complete your flying course. A huge bonus of paying as you go is that you do not have the debt after obtaining your pilot licence.

If you want to learn to fly take some time to write out your reason, it could be a family holiday, a new career, or the sheer joy of being in the air. Whatever the reason, these are the visions you need to focus on when any of the resisting thoughts arise. If you are physically able to learn to fly, it all comes down to how willing you are to make it happen. It is time to take the next step towards that dream.

CHAPTER 8

FASTEN YOUR SEATBELT – THE AIRLINE TRANSPORT PILOT LICENCE (ATPL)

In an earlier chapter, I mentioned how people approach me and say, "I want to get a Commercial Pilot Licence." Then, when I ask about the integrated or the non-integrated CPL they tend not to have any idea what I mean. The ATPL is also a common ask of potential pilots. The statement "I want to get the Airline Transport Pilot Licence" is likely to mean their end goal is to be an airline pilot. They understand the ATPL is the licence they require to do this. They are correct, but unfortunately these couple of sentences are usually the sum of knowledge and understanding. There is nothing wrong with the ambition to become an airline pilot however walking into a flight school with zero hours and walking out with an ATPL is not how the system works. Sadly, this is a common misunderstanding of would-be pilots who don't fully understand the process to gain an ATPL.

The Left Seat

So, what is an ATPL? An ATPL allows you to be a captain of an aircraft with a certain size and weight. The most common place where this is used is in the left seat of an airliner. This is a worthy ambition and common dream for many future pilots however there are a few steps required along the way.

The first step and most common pathway towards an ATPL is to start with a CPL, it does not matter whether you studied the integrated or non-integrated course.

An ATPL has a minimum requirement of 1500 hours. Even completing the non-integrated CPL, a pilot will only have 200 hours. So where do the remaining 1300 hours come from? Up until your CPL each hour of flying you have completed will have been paid for. It is unlikely that you will be able to afford the next 1300 hours of flying experience out of your own pocket. You will need to find employment after your CPL, remember, the CPL is your first point of entry into working as a commercial pilot. Over time you will build up the experience and hours towards the 1500-hour minimum requirement. If you were fortunate to be the minimum age of 18 when you obtained your CPL, you will have to wait until you are 21 to hold the ATPL.

The 1500 hours are broken down further into specific types of flying. It includes 100 hours of flying at night and 75 hours of flying on instruments. There are 7 theory subjects and a flight test required to complete the ATPL.

When you finished your CPL, you may only have a licence to fly around under the day Visual Flight Rules. To gain the night experience, you will need either a Night VFR rating or and Instrument rating. Your employer and the type of operations they undertake are likely to determine which of these ratings you undertake.

Jake gained employment straight after his CPL test in a small regional town that had seasonal tourism flights and some occasional passenger

Fasten Your Seatbelt - The Airline Transport Pilot Licence (ATPL)

and freight charter. After 12 months he returned to study and gained his instrument rating in the off season. This rating allowed him to fly on instruments and at night. With the seasonal work it took him 3 years to gain the flying experience requirements for the ATPL but there was still more to do.

There is a regulatory limit of flying hours that a pilot can fly in a 12-month period set generally at a maximum of 900 (there may be some exceptions). On paper, 1500hrs would equate to 18 months of flying to obtain, however in practice this is often not the case as pilots may not be flying the maximum hours in their first job after the CPL.

There is a flight test for the ATPL. The pilot undertaking this test should be well practiced in flight tests and proficiency checks as they will have likely completed several since they first started flying. The flight test is required to be in either a multi-engine turbine powered aircraft which could be operated multi crew, or it could be in an approved flight simulator for the larger type aircraft up to airliner jets.

The flight test is conducted under the IFR rules so current proficiency in IFR flying is a must for the flight test.

It is common for the pilot to not have had experience in the specific type of aircraft the ATPL flight test is in, so they will need to conduct a course of training in the aircraft to be proficient.

Before taking the ATPL flight test there are some additional requirements.

A pilot needs to have completed a Multi-Crew Coordination course (MCC). These courses are conducted at a flight training organisation. Each course is approved by the Civil Aviation Safety Authority for the specific flight training organisation. An instructor who teaches the course must have a minimum of 100 hours multi-crew experience, flying in a multi-crew environment. It is more likely the instructor will have significantly more experience than the minimum 100 hours.

The length of the MCC course will depend on the flight training organisation. Courses can vary between two to four weeks. An airline cadet pilot is likely to complete an MCC course as part of their cadetship in preparation for entering the airline.

ATPL Theory

Remember when I talked about the different subjects you had to complete for the CPL? The ATPL has a similar series of seven subjects however the information is geared around larger airline aircraft requirements. The subjects include:

Subject	Exam duration	Pass percentage
Meteorology	1.5 hours	70
Human Performance	1.25 hours	70
Navigation	1.5 hours	70
Aerodynamics & Aircraft Systems	1.5 hours	70
Flight Planning	3.0 hours	70
Performance & Loading	2.5 hours	70
Air law	1.5 hours	80

Similar to the CPL subjects the ATPL exams also have an expiry. When all the exams are completed within the required time frame they are permanently valid. If a commercial pilot has completed the theory examinations but does not meet all the other requirements, a phrase that is used in the USA is the "frozen ATPL". It is not technically an official term in Australia, although still widely used.

There is a fair amount involved in meeting the requirements of an ATPL, and not all of it is completed by attending a course. Much of the flying to gain the required hours is undertaken whilst a pilot is employed as a commercial pilot.

Fasten Your Seatbelt – The Airline Transport Pilot Licence (ATPL)

Here is a stepped approach:

- CPL (gain experience towards 1500 hours)
- Instrument rating (gain required experience towards 1500 hours)
- Theory course (can be self-study or part-time or full-time course for each subject
- Pass seven theory exams
- Complete MCC course
- Undertake aircraft type training (if not familiar with aircraft you have to take the ATPL flight test)
- Pass ATPL flight test in aircraft or flight simulator

How Does This Work in Practice?

Most non-airline cadet CPL holders will start with increasing their hours whilst working and obtain the instrument rating either before employment or during their employment after gaining additional flying experience.

If the pilot did not complete the ATPL theory subjects as an extension to their CPL course, they often self-study the easier subjects and then enrol in a course for the harder subjects. Pilots are often still working whilst completing this study. When pilots are approaching or even after they reach the required hours, they may enrol in a MCC course. These courses are more often full-time so the working pilot will need take leave to complete.

The final stage is preparation for the flight test and, depending on where the pilot is working and what type of aircraft they are flying, this may involve an aircraft type specific rating in a plane or simulator before being able to pass the ATPL flight test.

Whether a simulator or aircraft, both are expensive, that is why many pilots won't actually bother to go through this procedure up to the flight test. Individual pilots ensure they meet all the requirements and wait until they are hired by an airline. It is commonplace for the airline to take their pilots through this process in the type of aircraft the airline operates. There are pilots who complete this under their own volition however, more so to work with a specific employer rather than a "nice to have" credential.

Returning to Jake's story, he took three years post CPL to gain the required hours for the ATPL. He was fortunate his employer operated several night freight runs parallel to the daytime tourism business so Jake could achieve the required break down of night and instrument hours for the ATPL. Jake opted to take leave once again in the quieter season and enrolled in a full-time ATPL theory course, he had already started studying the subjects but had not taken any examinations. After the exams were passed, he returned to work another busy tourist season. Jake moved on to flying more advanced aircraft in the company and the next step would be the multi crew environment. He enrolled in an MCC course to give himself the competitive edge over other pilots who were also applying to the airlines. This wasn't mandatory before starting with the airline, however he figured he could benefit from the extra knowledge even with his current employer. He gained employment in an airline and the flight test for ATPL was eventually completed as part of his employment.

Another system of training and pathway to becoming an airline pilot is the Multi Crew Pilot Licence or MPL. This method of training is associated with cadet pilots training specifically for entry into an airline.

This chapter has focused on the ATPL and the pre-requisite of 1500 hours based on a person gaining a CPL and then gathering experience like Jake over several years to then qualify for the ATPL.

Fasten Your Seatbelt - The Airline Transport Pilot Licence (ATPL)

An MPL is airline specific training, if I used the analogy that I could teach someone to fly an A330 in a simulator from scratch (and spend more time and focus on all the idiosyncrasies and learnings around the A330), I would have a much more proficient pilot than one who learned to fly in a light aircraft and gained experience up to the ATPL by conducting local tourist joy flights for 1300 plus hours. After the first 100 hours, the pilot may be deemed to know all they can about how to fly that particular aeroplane on that particular route, but what would they know about the A330 and would those extra 1200 hours doing the same thing over and over equate to valuable flying experience?

The MPL takes a pilot with zero flying experience and trains them to be an airline pilot from scratch. Instead of a CPL the pilot obtains an MPL. The training will teach the pilot how to operate in a two-pilot operation in contrast to the standard CPL that teaches a pilot to operate single pilot. There is more time spent in simulators simulating emergencies that a pilot in a CPL course would not get to experience. More simulator time can also mean a shorter course time as weather dependency decreases.

In any standard flight training the weather plays an important role with respect to potential delays. The solo flight time in the MPL is minimal which is envisaged to minimise the gaining of any bad habits. The MPL course is associated with an airline so that when the pilot completes the course, they can be employed by the airline. The MPL does not allow the pilot to fly outside of the airline multicrew environment. The training a pilot completes in the MPL is specific to the airline they are going to work for. If a pilot didn't become employed by the airline and wanted to fly as a commercial pilot, they would need to complete an additional flight test for the CPL. It is likely that the pilot undertaking this exercise would need to complete some additional training in VFR single pilot operations.

Once a pilot has an MPL, it's the equivalent point of entry to the first job just like the CPL, however the MPL first job would be in an airline. After you finish the MPL course, you are qualified for multi crew operations in the specific type aircraft.

What is a Type Rating?

When a pilot learns to fly, they learn in a small aircraft it could be a Cessna 172 or Piper Warrior. It doesn't really matter which one, for when they receive their licence it does not specify the aircraft they can fly other than single engine class or later in their training it could be multi-engine class.

When it comes to larger aircraft, the pilot is type rated on each aircraft. Let's take some of the common airliners as examples. A pilot who can fly a Boeing 737 would have taken a course of training to be able to fly this specific aircraft. This Boeing 737 type rated pilot would not be permitted to fly an Airbus 320 aircraft. To do this, they would need to have taken training on the Airbus 320 and gain a type rating on that specific aircraft.

A pilot who is enrolled in an MPL course would have completed the type rating for the specific aircraft that the airline they are to be employed with operates as part of their course.

A commercial pilot like Jake could also complete a type rating at his own expense if he chose to. This would involve attending a course conducted by a simulator centre which would include both theory on the aircraft and its operations and flying the aircraft in the simulator. I mentioned earlier that it is uncommon for pilots in Australia to undertake type training as an individual as they wait until they are employed in an airline and are trained by the airline.

Type rating training is expensive and if the airline is paying for the type rating they may have some form of bond or return of service that is required to be paid by the pilot if they leave the airline before the due time.

Fasten Your Seatbelt – The Airline Transport Pilot Licence (ATPL)

An ATPL is a goal for the beginner pilot but is difficult to calculate the significant cost.

I am often asked, "If I get an ATPL can I work overseas?" The simple answer is yes with respect to the licence. The licence you hold is recognised by the International Civil Aviation Organisation (ICAO), a global body that manages the administration and governance of the convention on International Civil Aviation (Chicago Convention). Australia is a signatory to what we call the ICAO Annex 1, just as the US and UK and many other member states. This international membership means that National Aviation Authority of the USA or another member state would recognise the training that has been conducted in Australia and vice versa. If a person came to Australia with a USA based pilot licence the training would be recognised because of this arrangement.

Recognising the training is one part of the process. The National Aviation Authority may require some form of conversion process be completed to validate the licence. This will depend on which country however there is likely to be a theory examination/s and a flight check with an examiner to validate the licence.

Note: The earlier forms of licence such as PPL and CPL also have conversion processes under similar arrangements.

CHAPTER 9

WHO ARE YOU GOING TO CALL? CHOOSING A FLIGHT SCHOOL

Not every flight school is for everyone. If you think about kindergartens, primary schools, and secondary schools, parents often shop around to select the one that suits their child best. Different people thrive in different environments, so it is important that you do your research and find a school that will best fit you and your goals. The wrong choice could cost you in many ways. It is important you select the flight school that can provide the training you require.

How Do You Find the Right Flight School?

We talked about different airports at the beginning of the book. Flight schools, by nature, are located at the airport, as that is where they must operate from. To start with most people may look on the internet and gather some information but that is only part of the process. The next move should be to take a visit to the airport and knock on the door of each flight school. You owe it to yourself to knock on the door of all of the flight schools and see what they have to offer. You need to get a feel for what the flight school's about. You can ask them questions face to face. It is a good idea to have a written list of questions you have prepared earlier as this way you can gather the same information from each flying school to enable you to make an easier comparison.

Before I expand on the steps to assist you in finding a flight school, I want to highlight some subtle points that can often be overlooked.

In your visit to the airport, you will discover that there are small, medium and large flight schools. Some flight schools may operate under the banner of an Aero Club, these are operated by a committee of management, can be very social, and have a club type atmosphere. There are some flight schools that primarily offer commercial pilot training and have large volumes of full-time commercial students. In this type of environment, the social aspect such as sitting down, having a chat, talking about flying outside of your lesson, may be something that does not necessarily happen with that style of flight school. This is the reason why you need to gain a sense of what the flight school is like.

It is not only the flight school you need to review. You need to think about yourself, what do you want to achieve and how do you learn best. Remember, large schools, with large numbers, the logistics, are enormous. Organising a large cohort of students to be trained with weather and other variables, there must be a lot of processes in place to enable that to happen efficiently. I mentioned in the integrated CPL chapter, that in large flight schools it can be compared to hopping on a conveyor belt, to keep up with the pace. But if you hop off, for whatever reason, that conveyor belt keeps moving. If you do not have a disciplined learning regime, you may find that it is difficult to catch up so this type of organisation may not suit you.

Conversely, if you love and are looking for structure, it could be the perfect way in which you can achieve what you want and gain a CPL.

Who Are You Going to Call? Choosing a Flight School

Now, if somebody wanted to do the course super-fast (I'd first ask what the rush is as you want to enjoy this process), on paper, the integrated CPL course looks like it's the quickest way and as mentioned above if you thrive in structure this is often the most popular choice. I'd like to open your mind up to the possibility that you could complete the course just as fast taking a non-integrated CPL course pathway. Remember, when you have control of your own scheduling, and not the flight school having control over yours and your 29 classmates' schedule, you may find that you can get through in the same amount of time, potentially paying as you go, and with a little more flexibility. This would also accommodate opportunities such as landing on remote grass airstrip or going away for the weekend. You would have that flexibility to gain those hours, and you're not competing with your other 29 classmates.

Some of the questions you could ask would be completion rates of courses. How many students do they have in each class? What is the allocation of instructors to students? Often people ask what is the average age of the instructors, or is there a level of maturity and experience with their instructors? The age of an instructor does not necessarily equate to the flying experience of the instructor, so don't let your thinking become biased towards the type of instruction you could receive. Many times, I have heard, "Oh, I don't want some young, fresh instructor. I want somebody who is a little older and mature." Of course, I appreciate this comes down to personal preference, however you may find the young gun to be keen and enthusiastic, whereas the older instructor is tired and lacking interest. There are also impressions given that some flight instructors are only instructing to build their hours. The nature of the industry often puts flight instruction as the entry level for a pilot's first paid job. I like to think of this as the foundation stone to their career and it is important to get it right. Students benefit from this determination of new instructors wanting to get it right. In my experience a student quickly works out if an instructor is there for themselves and not the student, if you detected this, it's time to change instructors. Therefore, having a variety of instructors to facilitate any changes would be advantageous.

The Left Seat

The student-instructor relationship is key to productive learning. Ideally, it would be preferable to find the best matched instructor for you from the beginning of your training. If you want to change flight instructors, this is okay, however a word of warning: if you continually swap instructors for fit, like trying on shoes, this could be detrimental to your training in the early stages. It is said that we teach the way we learn so finding an instructor that has a similar learning style to you could promote a better learning environment. It is important to have a student instructor balance. I have instructed and overseen the instruction of many students. Sometimes, the changing of an instructor can make all the difference. It is important from the start that you know this is an option if needed.

Now that I have covered some of the subtle points that you should think about when selecting a school, you can move to more of the mechanics of finding a flying school.

Decide On Your Goal – Private or Commercial?

You first need to decide on training you want to take. This should be easier now you have read the earlier chapters and have a better understanding of the different courses. Do you want to complete a PPL and fly only for recreation? Or do you want to fly for a career and complete a CPL? Remember, even if you know you want to complete a PPL and think you may at some stage want to go further to the CPL you don't have to make that decision straight away. Similarly, if you enrol in a CPL course, and then decide that a PPL is all you want, you can stop part of the way through with only the PPL.

Note: Some of the integrated courses are designed to take you through to CPL and skip the PPL test. The training towards the PPL still counts if you stop halfway. You would need to speak with the flight school or possibly change flight schools to arrange the flight test for the PPL once you meet the requirements.

Who Are You Going to Call? Choosing a Flight School

So, You Want to be a Private Pilot?

If you decide you want a PPL, you don't need to look at a university course or diploma course for flying as these are geared towards the CPL. To complete your training for the PPL you will need to find a flight school that has a Part 141 approval certificate.

What Does a Part 141 or Part 142 Approval Mean For a Flight School?

A Part 141 school is a flight school that looks after most phases of pilot training. There are many different types of training that are incorporated under the Part 141 approval. The PPL is one of them. Part 141 is the rule set that relates to flying training organisations for a whole list of pilot training courses.

There is another rule set for a Part 142 school, which was covered in chapter 3 where I explained the 150-hour integrated CPL course. For someone who is enrolled in an integrated course, that must be completed at a flight school that is approved by the Civil Aviation Safety Authority as a Part 142 school.

It is likely the flight school conducting commercial pilot training that is a Part 142 school will also hold a Part 141 certificate for the training conducted outside the 150-hour integrated CPL syllabus. There is simulator training, and type rating training that also occurs under the Part 142, but at this stage you do not need to worry about this.

You may choose to gain a Recreational Pilot Certificate as discussed in chapter 2. This training needs to be completed at a Recreational Aviation Australia (RAAus) flying school. There are some cases where a Part 141 flying school may also be registered with RAAus and be able to offer this training. The RAAus training hours can count towards the RPL, PPL and CPL total hours

The Left Seat

Commercial Pilot - Integrated or Non-Integrated?

If you are going to undertake the integrated CPL course your options of flight schools is reduced. The flight training school needs to be a Part 142 flight school. In Chapter 3, we discussed in detail the integrated CPL. If this is your preference you then need to decide which programme you want to complete for the integrated CPL course. There is a selection of courses for you to decide. You can select a university degree over a three-year period, a diploma course which is between one to two years or an integrated CPL with only the CASA licence outcome over 12 to 18 months with no additional academic qualifications.

Once you have decided which design of integrated CPL, you need to make sure that you compare your options.

If you have read all the previous chapters, you will now have the tools to be able to compare each of the different courses. You will understand what you're comparing and be able to compare apples with apples.

You need to think about which course will suit you, your time, your goals, and your finances. Remembering that the university courses generally come with some form of government funding, or government loan system. Some diploma courses also come with government loans and there are also courses where you can pay as you go.

Then there's the 200-hour non-integrated commercial pilot course. The 200-hour CPL course can be completed at a flight school which has Part 141 training approval. The pathway you take for this course is flexible and can be discussed with the flight school.

As explained in chapter 4, this course can include a mix of training including RAAus flying hours or gliding hours. If you are looking at getting a job after your CPL, it is important to remember that most charter aircraft are not two seat light aircraft as found in RAAus. If

Who Are You Going to Call? Choosing a Flight School

you did take this route, you may benefit by utilising larger aircraft for the later parts of your training that may be more representative of the aircraft you are wishing to fly in your future employment. The more experience you have on completion of the CPL the more employable you will be to your future employer.

Aircraft Types and Availability

When reviewing potential flight schools, the aircraft they use to complete the training should be discussed with you. It is natural tendency for the flight school to be biased towards the aircraft they operate and there is nothing wrong with this. What you need to decide is are the aircraft suitable for the training you need to undertake, is there availability of the aircraft you want to fly in and are the aircraft well maintained. These are all questions the flight school should be happy to answer, if they don't want to discuss this you may think of looking elsewhere.

Location of the Flight School

In Australia, flight schools are located both near cities and in the regional areas. If you are looking at a university type flying course these are more commonly located in the major cities. Metropolitan airports can have several flights schools operating out of the one airport. Regional airports may only have one, possibly two, flight training schools that operate from them. Location is often a choice of convenience for the individual; however, don't be afraid to expand your search outside your local area as it is about finding a school that is the correct fit for you. You may ask some questions about where the local training area for the flight school is located as in some instances an aircraft may have to transit for some time to reach the area where they can commence their lesson. Time in the air is expensive, so you may choose to spend it in travel time on the ground instead.

Budget

You are investing in your flight training. As with any investment, the cost can be high. It is no secret that flying is not the cheapest activity. That doesn't mean you can't fly on a budget. When selecting a flight school, you need to make sure that when you are comparing prices that old saying that keeps coming up of comparing apples with apples applies. You need to check whether the price quoted is based on minimum hours or what would be considered average hours of the average pilot. To make prices sound lower most flights schools quote on minimum hours. This also allows an easy comparison of price. Next, you should ask about the number of average hours for the flight school's students, and the additional cost for the extra flying hours. When comparing prices, you also need to look at similar aircraft types as some aircraft are smaller and potentially more affordable to operate.

As there are landing fees at many airports, you should also ask if the hourly rate includes this fee or is it added on afterwards.

Whilst you are asking the flight school about the aircraft flying hours you may also like to enquire about the instructor briefing time. If the dual rate of training includes the pre-flight and post-flight briefs by the instructor or is this considered a separate cost.

Theory courses are also a consideration. Does the flight school conduct its own theory training courses? Are these invoiced separately and at what stage of the course are these undertaken?

Theory examination costs charged by CASA are going to be comparable however if paying for a theory course ensure you are aware whether exam fees are included in the course.

At the back of the book there is a pricing template to help you compare apples with apples

Payment Options

When you are discussing your course with the flight training organisation, you need to make sure you are clear on the payment options and if you are required to pay any monies in advance and understand the refund policy. The options available will vary between training organisations, from block payments, scheduled payments, and pay as you go.

If you are undertaking a course that attracts any form of government funding it is important to read through all the terms and conditions of the loan system so there are no surprises. It's not "free money" as I have heard many times. It will need to be paid back. The courses that do involve a government loan may have a component of the fees that are not part of the loan, so make sure you determine what these are before you commence the course.

What if I Want to Change My Course?

With any course, whether it be at a flight school, university, TAFE college or Registered Training Organisation, even if it is a full-time integrated course, there are always options to leave. Hopefully, there will not be the need to change courses. In the past I've had people come to me who are enrolled in a course and not receiving what they originally thought the course was about. This is not necessarily the fault of the training provider. Instead, it is because the student had different expectations of the course structure due to a lack of initial understanding of what they were signing up for. The student can often feel stuck and unsure of what they need to do to change course or flight school. It is a simple process for students to transfer between courses and flight training providers. The new flight school will transfer student records with the permission of the student.

Depending on the course, the student would need to look at the opt-out clauses in relation to credits and refunds. You may find that if you've paid money up front, opting out may cause you to forfeit your right to any funds that have already been paid. Or, if you're at a course that has government fee loan assistance, you may find that if you leave before completing the unit you are currently studying, you may forfeit the funds for that unit.

What if I was doing a PPL, and I decided I wanted to enrol in a CPL course that is a university course? Is that possible? You would need to check with the university first, but it has been done before. It will depend on the university as to how much of your previous flying training experience they will credit towards the course. Your flying hours and experience will always be there, it is more an academic decision as to what to credit.

Similarly, if you were enrolled in a university course and decided you didn't want to complete the university component and only wanted the licence. If this were the case, you could check with the flight school associated with the university to see if you can continue just the licence outcome and notify the university of your intention not to proceed. If this is not able to be facilitated by the flight school, then changing flight schools is an option. The new flight school would perform an assessment flight and then likely to pick up from where you left off or give you credit up to a specific entry point to their course.

The intention of this book is assist you in becoming acquainted with the technicalities and processes around the pilot's licence to enable you to make more informed decisions and remove some of the unseen hurdles you could encounter. The aim in this chapter is for you to make the best decision for *you*. I'm not here to tell you to attend my flight school. In fact, most of the time when I do speak to people that come in the door, I answer their questions, explain how it works, and then I say, "While you're at the airport, please take a walk around, visit the other flight schools. Find out what, they offer, and then make your decision. I am here if you have further questions."

Who Are You Going to Call? Choosing a Flight School

Doing your homework can save you so much time and agony. There's nothing worse than having that passion of wanting to learn to fly quashed when it's met by the hurdle of an unsuitable flight school. In this instance there is often some loyalty to your flight instructor, however inside you know the flight school does not have your best interests in mind. It's human nature to persist a bit longer, too often I've seen this happen. The student convinces themselves by saying, "I'm really close to my licence, I'll just stay a little bit longer, because I'll just get over that hurdle." I see them six months later, and they're still in that same spot unfortunately no closer to achieving their goal.

If you ever find yourself in that position, I advise you to take a step back, and go back to the beginning. Ask yourself why you wanted to fly and what you wanted to achieve. If the flight school isn't providing what you need then speak with them as you are the customer. If you can't find a clear pathway forward, then you will need to make the decision to change. In flying training, the only thing we can't change is the weather. If I could do that, I wouldn't be in the flight school business and you could find me on a beach in the Bahamas.

I would like to think that everyone makes the right decision from the onset and this chapter is to help you with your deliberations. If you choose the right flight school at the beginning and know what you want to achieve this should minimise any issues along the way.

CHAPTER 10

LIGHT WINDS AND CLEAR SKIES – ENJOY THE JOURNEY

I want you to picture yourself high in the sky at the controls of an aeroplane. It doesn't really matter what type of aeroplane for this exercise. The sky is crystal blue, the winds are calm and the there is a comfortable warmth coming from the sun through the window. You can see the far horizon, and between you and the horizon is a familiar landscape. This is flying, this is what you are going to learn to do. This will become your journey and I want you to enjoy it.

I have now been flying for over 30 years. It was a childhood dream I had always held, which made it all the more satisfying to achieve. I want to acknowledge that everyone's journey is different and that I am yet to meet anyone who has taken the steps to become a pilot without encountering challenges along the way. Even with challenges, for me it was, overall, an enjoyable experience. This chapter is a reminder that there can be challenges and it is not all easy, yet you want to make sure that you do take the time to enjoy the journey along the way.

A problem I see often is that people will be so career-orientated that they forget about the fun of flying. The intent of this book is to assist you in your research to becoming a pilot. I want you to make sure you are conscious of the traps of others who have gone before you, whether it be insufficient research or focusing so hard on the outcome that you missed some of the joys along the way.

Not everyone is comfortable with learning something new and learning to fly certainly feels novel. Both the skill of flying the aeroplane and the theory behind it can overwhelm the new student pilot. This feeling of overwhelm can be reduced, by the student and the instructor having clear expectations on what is required for each lesson and ample preparation time in between lessons for the student to prepare.

As a student, you don't only require preparation time you also need absorption time. This is time between lessons to take in what you have learnt, review it in your mind by re-enacting the lesson with visualisation, or as instructors call it "armchair flying." By taking this time to go over the lesson it will enhance your learning and reinforce some of the new skills and techniques you have been taught. Too often, I have heard stories of keen students dictating to the instructor they must do three lessons a day. In simple math terms, say it is 12 hours to solo (remember this is a numbers game) then it will be four days of flying and theoretically the student will be solo. I am not saying this is impossible, however given the amount of theory learning and understanding that is required if they had no previous experience, they are unlikely to achieve this. Therefore, it is important to set clear expectations. My observations with students in the early phases of flight or with any new phases of flight being taught is they experience fatigue from information overload as the flight progresses, impacting their learning.

Flying is a good leveler. Remember at school where you had those people who were good at studying and always ended up with high marks. Then you had those who chose an apprenticeship because they were good with their hands. Learning to fly will test you in both areas. Henry Ford said, *"If you think you can or you think you can't you're right."* It is important to be open minded about your abilities if you want to succeed at being a pilot. You do not want the preconceived opinions of others or yourself to prevent you from achieving your dream or from having fun whilst achieving it.

It would be true to say that in my experience of teaching people to fly the majority of learners prefer the flying component of the training over the theory component. Flying is not just about theory or just about flying - it's a blend of both. Student pilots need to understand that it is a combination of knowledge and skills that are required to make up the entire pilot licence package. It is quite common to see a student who is struggling with the theory component use the flying like a carrot as a reward to the efforts put in for the theory study.

CELEBRATE THE ACHIEVEMENTS - FIRST SOLO

"I had been doing circuits with the instructor for the last few lessons and we taxied into the runup bay where the instructor informed me that they were getting out and I could take the plane for a single circuit on my own. I was nervous but I knew this was what I had been training for, and I thought if my instructor figured I could do it, then they are the expert. I lined up the aircraft on the runway and was cleared for take-off as I moved the throttle forward and took my feet off the brakes the aircraft started rolling down the runway.

"The speed to take off came very quickly and as I gently pulled back on the controls the aircraft lifted into the air, it was much sooner than in the previous circuits. The aircraft climbed really well. My instructor had warned me that this would happen as the aircraft is much lighter with only one person on board. I carefully maintained the runway heading as I had been taught and climbed to the circuit altitude leveling out and making a radio call to get my traffic. I had to follow a Cessna on late down wind. I looked for the aircraft and saw it as it was turning onto base and then I remembered to do my prelanding checks. It was a surreal feeling on the downwind leg looking to my right and seeing no one sitting there. I took a deep breath and told myself to relax, as I knew what I had to do to land the aircraft.

"I turned onto base and made sure my traffic was well ahead and set up the aircraft for the landing just as my instructor had taught me. I spoke aloud to myself in the same words the instructor used. Checking my attitude and my airspeed I looked out and turned onto final I could see the aircraft in front of me landing on the runway. I continued to watch the attitude and was cleared to land. As I came over the runway, I adjusted my power and pulled back the controls so I could land on the main wheels, I don't remember the nose wheel touching down but it all felt pretty smooth to me. I taxied off the runway and back to the flight school and picked up my instructor along the way. I was pretty excited to think I had just flown an aircraft by myself, but it wasn't until later that day when I was watching other aircraft take off and land that I realised how amazing this feat really was."

This is an extract from a note one of my students wrote to me after they went solo for the first time. As they mentioned, it is an amazing feat, and they should ensure to treat it as such and celebrate their achievement.

Light Winds and Clear Skies – Enjoy the Journey

Other achievements are the first training area solo, where you take yourself from the aerodrome to the training area and return to the aerodrome, your RPL test or taking your first passenger. I recall my first passenger was my grandfather. When I was 14, I had saved up and arranged a joy flight during my school holidays. I needed a lift to the airport and called my grandfather to see if he wanted to go on a joy flight. The only catch was he needed to take me to the airport. That was my first flight in a light aircraft, and I promised him that when I had a licence I would take him flying. It took seven years and I took him flying a few days after I received my licence. It is moments like these you need to celebrate.

You should celebrate your theory examination achievements, each and every one of them. I watch students pass from one exam to the next as if they are in a race, rather than savouring the moment of achievement with their newfound knowledge. Some of this knowledge could save their life one day and its significance should not pass without recognition.

Every one of these steps is important and warrants due reflection - and a pat on the back. As a flight examiner, I have the privilege of being the first person to congratulate a student when they pass a flight test and remind them to go and celebrate. I am sometimes met with the rebuttal of, "I'm not there yet so will wait until I get there." Where is "there," you may ask? Well, it is always the next licence or the next rating. If you are waiting for this, you will never get there as there will always be someone who has more hours than you, more aircraft types than you, more ratings than you. Forget where they are and look at where you are now. Whether it be RPL, PPL, CPL or ATPL these are all significant milestones and are worthy of some additional self-praise.

Celebrating each of these achievements will help to sustain your enthusiasm and motivation for the next phase of training or the next flying adventure. Celebrating is not just about having a toast to what you have accomplished, it is about reflecting on how you arrived at where you are now and acknowledging the path you have taken. To succeed, you need commitment to try, try and try again. With this commitment, your belief and confidence in your ability will also grow and you will be able to harness this for your next steps.

Celebrating will help get you through the parts of the training you find difficult. I don't believe there is such a thing as a natural born pilot but there are people that appear to pick up the skills more quickly than others. Just because they appear to be good at it doesn't mean they don't have challenges too. In conversations with these students, I've found a common thread, they all adhere to similar practices, which is a commitment to be consistent in their efforts. Consistently applying themselves to the learning tasks makes for a great student. There's that saying, "to start you need to be committed to finish you need consistency," a good motto for your flying training.

Don't become one of those students who become so focused on the process of achieving their licence that they lack the willingness to even entertain the idea of a small celebration as an acknowledgment of their achievement. These students often lack confidence in their abilities and fall into the "forever a student" cycle, they are always adding new aircraft types, ratings and endorsements to their licence but not ever actually using them. It is noble to always want to learn and there's nothing wrong with this. As an instructor I am always encouraging my students and fellow instructors to learn new things and enhance their knowledge and skills. However, remember to celebrate the achievement and use it. If you are a private pilot you did this for a reason, it could be to take friends flying, it could be to go away for weekends, it could be because you wanted to conquer a fear of flying. Whatever your reason, remember the "why", and when you achieve your goal, celebrate.

Now, I would like to think you have heard the message to celebrate along the way as this celebration will ensure you appreciate and enjoy your hard-earned efforts. When you start flying, I want to you return and re-read this chapter after each of your milestones.

Use It or Lose It

Once you have your pilot licence it is important for you to use it. The longer you go between practicing the skill of flying the less proficient you are going to be performing it. This sounds obvious, however it is surprising how many pilots obtain their licences and then other things in their life get in the way of them flying. As expected, this is more prevalent in PPL holders than commercial pilots as the CPL holder, once employed, is flying as part of their profession. In earlier chapters you read about some of the trips pilots have taken with their various licences and ratings. I would like to think that you too could enjoy some of these into the future as pilot in command.

There was something that originally sparked your interest in wanting to learn to fly. You made the commitment of time and effort to obtain the licence and an investment of this magnitude in yourself needs to be used. With a PPL you can fly all around Australia. The vastness of the country means that there are endless opportunities for pilots to fly and explore. Whether you are flying for recreation or as part of your hours building (as was mentioned in the 200-hour CPL course) every day that you go flying you will be gaining further experience and skills. Using your licence is integral to the continual learning process and is part of enjoying the journey.

In a day where people are conscious of who they may be travelling with for the fear of picking up a virus, taking your friends and family on a holiday can bring greater peace of mind.

There are some incredible places to see via air travel in Australia and gaining your pilot's licence opens up the door to you and your friends and family. Imagine taking your friends for a long weekend to Lake Eyre when it is in flood. During this time, Lake Eyre has plenty of tourists visiting, specifically to take a scenic flight over the lake. With a PPL, you have the ability to fly yourself around the lake. How awesome is that? Maybe a flight to a winery that has its own accommodation and restaurant on site for the weekend or fly into that airshow you have been attending for years.

You could plan your trip of a lifetime around Australia. The Blue Mountains, Byron Bay, Sunshine Coast, Cairns, Mt Isa, Kakadu, Broome, Rottnest Island, Exmouth, the Nullabour, the Barossa, Cradle Mountain, the Great Ocean Road. The opportunities to explore the country and have some serious enjoyment are only limited by your imagination.

Earlier, I mentioned that there are always more ratings, aircraft, and endorsements that you can add on to your licence. When you are looking at some of the add-ons, think about the different ones you can undertake to enhance your skill. We talked about those a little bit earlier, use these as an opportunity to have some fun.

Learning aerobatics is one such add-on. For some, that might seem terrifying, but for others, it seems fun and a way to further hone their skills. Learning formation so you can fly alongside other aircraft is another example of upskilling whilst creating enjoyment of flying with other people.

It is possible that not every flight will personally give you the buzz of enjoyment, rather it can often be more the joy that you bring other people when you take them flying. When they love it you will feed off of their enthusiasm.

When you have a pilot's licence, don't put it on the shelf. See it as an achievement and make sure you do use it and make the effort to plan to use it.

There are many aviation organisations to join as soon as you start flying. I have included a list at the back of the book. These organisations will have different events and opportunities to fly away with other pilots. Becoming part of an organisation with likeminded people is a big incentive and helps keep you motivated and encouraged to go flying. There's nothing better than everybody flying away for a weekend, enjoying the weekend, then flying home. These are lasting memories that will be talked about for years.

A note of warning: as a pilot, sometimes you might find some non-pilots are not as interested in your conversation as you may think. However, they usually tend to listen politely to ensure they don't ruin their chances of an invite on your next adventure because they'd like to experience the joys of getting to their destination quicker with you.

For the Commercial Pilot Trainees

As discussed earlier, if you are enrolled in a 150-hour integrated course, there are less opportunities for you to explore the PPL phase, as you will be required to complete the navigation exercises as mapped out by the flight training school. Any variations to the command time in the 150-hour course will need to be approved. If you are taking the 200-hour course route you are likely to have the ability to experience some of the PPL opportunities as part of your command building hours. We are the sum of our total experiences so make sure you plan your hour building time to maximise your experience towards the CPL and beyond.

For Those Who Want to be an Airline Pilot

Unless you are an airline cadet there will be various jobs along the pathway to an airline, I want you to make sure that you enjoy the journey along the way. Once you have a CPL and are being paid to fly, the choice of destinations becomes limited by your employer and customer, but the choice of employer is something you still have some control over.

The Left Seat

There may be several employers in your aviation career and each one is adding to your experience and future goals to become an airline pilot. It is important that in each level of employment you give of your best. The aviation industry in Australia is small. Some pilots unexpectedly find their preferred employer during this journey.

I'd like to leave you with this anecdote, which is often mentioned in aviation circles among pilots new and old.

There is a pilot who is flying in a small Cessna training aircraft (after reading chapter 5 you know what that is) and they are in the circuit. The circuit is the rectangular pattern we fly in and out of the airport. This pilot is in the circuit pattern between 1000 feet and the ground. This pilot looks up and they see a slightly larger aeroplane, a multi-engine aeroplane, flying a couple of 1000 feet higher than them. This multi-engine aeroplane is performing different manoeuvres over the aerodrome. The Cessna pilot looks up and thinks, "I've only just started my flying, I'd really love to fly that that multi-engine aeroplane one day, that would be so cool."

We then go to the pilot flying in the multi-engine aeroplane. That multi-engine aeroplane pilot has been flying a bit longer than the Cessna pilot. On the frequency, they hear the voice from a pilot in a regional airliner. Looking in the distance they can see the small turbo prop airliner is positioning for an approach to the airport. The multi-engine pilot thinks to themselves, "I'm doing all this training right now because I need to increase my hours for my next step, I want to fly for that regional airline."

We step into the cockpit of that turbo prop regional airliner. The pilot is busy preparing the aeroplane for the approach and looks up as they can hear an aircraft on another frequency. There's an airline jet overhead. This jet is on an international flight. The turbo prop pilot looks up and thinks, "With all the time in this turbo prop aeroplane, I'm getting closer now to my goals of an international airline pilot, another six months and I can apply for my dream job."

Light Winds and Clear Skies - Enjoy the Journey

Let's now jump to the flight levels of our international airliner. We look into the somewhat larger cockpit and see the captain, sitting comfortably at the controls with his cup of coffee chatting with his first officer. He looks down at the small aerodrome they are passing over and the first officer mentions that he once took lessons there. The captain spotted the small Cessna in the circuit turning final and comments, "I wish I was down there, hand-flying some circuits."

It does not matter so much where you are, whether you are high up or low down, or in the early or latter stages of your flying career, there's always something to aspire to. Whatever your flying aspiration, make sure you enjoy the journey and not just focus on arriving at your destination.

If you have made the decision to learn to fly, congratulations. When you attain your pilot licence, make sure to pat yourself on the back as you will have joined the 1% of the population who have mastered the skill of flying an aeroplane.

CHAPTER 11

STAY IN CONTROL – SAFETY

"Is it safe to fly aeroplanes?" This question is one I frequently receive from people who are fearful of flying. You have probably heard that flying is safer than driving a car. I am not going to go into statistics, but you will find if you did that it is correct. Most people will drive their car to the airport before they go and fly in an aeroplane, making the risk higher on the drive than the flight. Out of the seven common fears – criticism, poverty, failure, death, offending others, looking foolish or fear of success – I suspect those fearing flying are sitting high on the fear of death list. It is more common to die from falling out of bed than in an aeroplane accident, but I don't think the average person fears going to bed at night.

Fears are real to the individual experiencing them and for those who do have them about flying my previous paragraph will provide little solace. If you do have a fear of flying, I suggest you speak to someone who deals in this area of expertise if you wish to overcome it. For students learning to fly to overcome their fear of flying, this is just one part of their strategy.

Back to Safety

Safety in aviation is one of the things we take seriously as a professional, an organisation and an industry. I mentioned at the beginning of the book that the industry was highly regulated, it is not the regulations that provide the safety, but they do form part of the safety net. The aviation industry is a much younger industry than the maritime and rail industries, as it was only 1903 when the Wright brothers first took flight. In the early years of aviation, the industry was very reactive. When an accident occurred, the information would filter across the world and the national aviation authorities and associated aviation entities would learn from the accident. This still happens today but as the industry has developed, so has its focus on safety and safety culture, making it considerably more proactive when it comes to safety.

The reactive nature can be witnessed when there is an accident or incident. If an incident occurs in an aircraft, whether it be a component failure, ATC failure or pilot training failure to name a few, it is investigated thoroughly. The outcomes of this thorough investigation are broadcast across the industry, in order for changes to be made. Some of the changes are advisory, while some are mandated by regulation.

This process is not just local within the country of origin where an incident takes place, it is much broader and occurs globally. When there are issues related to specific aircraft types, where an incident has occurred you will find the wheels are set in motion across the world to ensure that another similar incident will not occur. No system is perfect as we have seen in more recent times with the Boeing 737 MAX aircraft. I am sure regulators and airline manufactures have learned from this experience.

Aviation accidents are still head-turners and in the media there remains a fascination with aeroplanes creating that air of mystique. If there is an accident, it will be broadcast all over the news. If we take the Australian news as an example. If Qantas, the Australian national carrier, has an aeroplane with a sick passenger on board, or there is an unexpected warning light, and as a result they turn back and return to the point of departure you can be assured this will make the news. There is no one hurt, but because of the nature of the news cycle, it seems that everybody needs to know about it on the six o'clock news.

Contrary to this, there may have been a five-car pile-up on the motorway in which four people have been killed, but you will find this may only make the first run of the six o'clock local news and not even on every channel. The unwaning novelty of aviation makes it newsworthy, and the stories about it are often sensationalised, even though the event may be almost routine and not unsafe. You need to put a filter through the broadsheet news, because the media hype can be quite significant, particularly on a slow news day.

Safety and professionalism are instilled in pilots from day one of their flight training. There are many parts that contribute to the overall safety of every flight. Pilots have medicals to ensure they are fit and healthy, professional pilots have flight and duty times to ensure they are not fatigued, the aircraft have to be checked by maintenance engineers and signed off suitable for flight, and the air traffic controllers who control the aircraft also have to be medically fit and trained. It is a requirement of flight schools with integrated training courses to have a safety management system and safety manager. The safety management system will require specific reporting and investigation of any accidents, incidents or systems to ensure continued safety across the organisation.

A few years ago, I had the privilege of being principal for a day at a local secondary school. During the course of the day, the senior students had been visited by the road safety advisors. Many of these students had learner permits and were now building their hours towards their driver licence. I was asked by one of the students how many hours it takes to get a pilot licence. Before answering I threw the question back to the rest of the class. These students had just been listening to how to get a driver's licence in Victoria, Australia. They required 120 hours, including 20 hours at night, of supervised driving before they were eligible to take the driver test. Based on the knowledge they had on driving and with the assumption that flying a plane must be much harder, most of the answers shouted out by the students were well above the 120 with some answering up to 400 hours. When I said 40 hours for a PPL they all looked at me astounded at such a small amount. I would say it is more 55 on average but even so it is less than half of the 120 hours required for a driver's licence.

We know through various advertising campaigns there are many issues about young drivers. If you have ever tried to insure a car for a young person this will be reinforced by the price due to the increased risks of accidents with young drivers. These risks have also added additional restrictions on our P plate drivers based on their age and inexperience.

A person is permitted to fly an aeroplane solo at 15 years old under the supervision of a flight instructor. They can gain their first licence, a RPL, where they can carry passengers at 16 years old. At 17 years old, they can gain a PPL and take passengers all over Australia.

I often ask myself why is that the case, when these students are too young to hold a car licence. I believe a lot of this comes down to the training. A good friend of mine who is also a pilot and I have had long discussions about this and are of the opinion that if we taught our children to drive using the same approach we do to learning to fly a plane they would be much safer.

Before each flight, the pilot will inspect the aircraft as per a checklist to ensure that the aircraft is suitable and safe to fly. The aircraft must undergo routine inspections by LAMEs, who themselves have undergone years of training to gain the privileges of their licences. All registered aircraft must be maintained to specific standards. There are many old aircraft still in service and this is because of the strict maintenance schedules they have been required to be maintained in accordance with.

Stay in Control – Safety

The aircraft may be senior in years, but it is a little like your grandpa's axe, it has had a new handle and a new blade but not at the same time. Older aircraft are often like this, they are technically the same aircraft, but most parts have been replaced at some point in its lifetime.

In comparison to learning to drive a car, when learning to fly a plane there is a lot of time spent on handling emergencies which all adds to the safety of the flight.

In larger aircraft there are lots of systems and lots of redundancy built into those systems to ensure that if there is a failure of some description, the backup system is designed to activate to minimise the impact of the failure. Pilots spend a lot of time learning about these systems, how they work and how the backup systems work in the event of a failure. Pilots also spend many hours learning and practising what to do in the case of various emergency situations. Undertaking this training and demonstrating competency at this is a reoccurring practice throughout a pilot's flying life.

Most pilots are fortunate that they never get to exercise all this training for real, but they understand why it is there and know it's there if they need it. All this training adds to the safety of the flight and the safety of the industry.

When I learnt to drive a car, I don't remember covering emergencies thoroughly like I did when learning to become a pilot and I certainly wasn't tested on them.

If you want to become a pilot, it is likely that you won't be the one worried about the safety of it. More often than not, you will have to convince someone close to you that your desire to fly is not a risky prospect. When someone asks me what I do and I respond with, "I teach people to fly," you would be amazed at how many people have said to me, "Aren't you scared?" Obviously not, but this is an indication of where their own feelings and thoughts lay on the matter.

The Left Seat

If you have a close friend or relative that is concerned about you learning to fly for safety reasons that you feel are not valid, you may choose to educate them in response to their fears, and remember these are their fears, not yours.

Over the years of training young pilots, I have seen parents often worry about their child going flying. As a parent I completely understand the concern you can have for a child. I have found that once I take the time to sit down and explain how the system works, they feel much more at ease with the whole situation. In their minds they have a child who they can't get to mow the lawn or do the dishes or even make their bed competently. With this in mind, they can't possibly see how they could fly a plane. This book would be a good place to start answering your questions, and I would also suggest sitting down with an instructor to get any additional concerns answered. An understanding of what is involved generally leads to more confidence in the process.

This is not limited to parents and children. It could be any significant person in your life that may need to be reassured that you will be safe.

There are wonderful shows on television that, as pilots, we all enjoy, such as *Air Crash Investigation*. Unfortunately, those who worry about flight safety will pick all the bad things out of these shows to support their argument, just as I can discuss the good things that come out of the investigations, such as education on the preventative systems, regulations or practices that have come into play since the accident or incident, demonstrating how the industry continually improves.

I encourage you to do your own homework and research which flight school you want to train at. You should raise these issues with the flight school, and they will be able to respond to your questions and concerns.

Overall, the industry is made up of highly skilled people, who from day one of their training are being influenced by and taught safe practices and culture. When you start your training you too will become part of that culture in the wonderful industry that is aviation.

CHAPTER 12

FROM THE CLASSROOM TO THE SKY - AVIATION VET IN SCHOOL

Start your career early. If you are like me and have always dreamed of being a pilot from a young age, there is the availability to start flying as part of your school studies.

There are more and more schools offering STEM subjects and aviation often arises as a subject in these classes. Most states in Australia will have a secondary school that offers a course in aviation in some format. It may be an elective or year-long subject, and there is even a dedicated aviation high school in one state.

If you are keen on aviation and becoming a pilot, but don't want to be the odd person who likes planes, ensure you do your research as you may be able to find a secondary school that has aviation in its curriculum.

The Left Seat

If you are at a school that has a Vocational Education and Training curriculum (VET) you could undertake an aviation qualification or part thereof whilst at secondary school.

I wish that this type of study opportunity had been available when I was growing up as I may not have been thought of as that odd girl who wanted to fly aeroplanes. Even at school reunions after all these years, women come up to me and say, "I remember you were always into planes." Being part of the aviation industry now for many years has made me realise that I was not alone and there were others who felt that way too.

Aviation is a specialist area and, like many specialist areas, if you are not in the industry you may not know much about what is involved. I speak to many career teachers who, when approached by a student who wants to be a pilot, direct them to the Air Force or an Airline Cadetship. These are the good outcomes. On the other hand, students are often discouraged from pursuing aviation due to the lack of understanding on the part of the teachers when they ask for career guidance. Career advisors can't know about every career, but they do have an obligation to point the students in the right direction and not discourage them from their dreams no matter how impossible they may seem at the time. I've had students come to me saying their teacher told them blatantly that they don't have the math and physics marks to become a pilot. Responses like these and the one of my year 12 coordinator telling me that women are air hostesses and not pilots are not helpful. All of these comments are born from a lack of knowledge and information.

If you have read the rest of this book, you are well ahead of any unresearched teacher wishing to advise you on your future aviation career and should have the tools to further pursue your research.

We often see students at school doing accelerated studies to get a jump ahead on their next year. Taking an aviation VET course is akin to that as you are getting a head start on your chosen career. Even if you decide not to go all the way to a commercial pilot after school, you will still have experienced the wonders of flight and what it has to offer. There are many occupations in the aviation industry for which this experience can give you a good grounding.

In aviation theory the topics studied make practical sense and can also create greater understanding of other more dry academic subjects at school by giving practical applications to the knowledge taught.

There have been several times when I have taught a classroom of teenagers and their behavior is not much different to a class full of primary school students. However, when those individual teenagers are one on one with their instructor in an aeroplane there is an astounding level of maturity. The environment and confidence gained in learning to fly a plane is something that I see carry over to other areas in the student's lives and studies.

What Does the Course Involve?

I will speak about the course I am involved with at Tristar. Throughout earlier chapters, I discussed the CPL and how it can be tied to the Diploma of Aviation to achieve a CPL. This diploma is a combination of 29 competency units. These units work in parallel with the units and elements of training that the CASA pilot training syllabus require.

Obviously, you cannot complete the entire diploma whilst in year 11 and 12 at school as you have to commit to you school studies, but you can take Aviation VET as a subject. The theory for the units is completed in the Wednesday afternoon VET timeslot for students, while the flying component is completed on the weekends and during school holidays. The course contains just over a third of the units required for the diploma which gives them a considerable head start to those who plan to enrol in courses post year 12.

The Left Seat

Enrolments for VET usually happen around October the year before when students are in year 10, so don't leave it too late, although there are some circumstances in which late enrolments are accepted. Many pilots I've trained have had the desire to fly an aeroplane since primary school. This opportunity is one they would have jumped at had it been available for them.

In all of my years of teaching students to fly, this course is the one where I have witnessed the greatest impacts in students' lives. It is not just me who has seen the difference - often, teachers or parents will call me to let me know how much of a difference the course has made to the student across all of their studies. Students are working harder and achieving results they never thought were possible.

One student who was at risk of dropping out of school, as they didn't show a lot of interest, convinced his teacher to let him do this course. The teacher's initial thought was it could be a waste of time and money as the student had not applied themselves in any other aspect of their schooling. However, the student's persistence paid off by convincing their teacher, who had never before seen this level of enthusiasm in the student. The student managed to convince their parents and was able to arrange an advance on some funds that they would have received for their birthday and started the course. The student proved themselves to be a model student by reaching all the milestones on time or ahead of schedule. It wasn't until the middle of the second year that the careers teacher contacted me to let me know how happy and proud she is of this student and to thank us for all we had done. Always willing to accept praise, I said thank you and asked what was it that she was so proud of. It turned out that the student was about to receive a most-improved award at school, but it carried more significance than that. The student had decided to set up a mentoring programme that identified students with no direction and help them find their path in life.

There have been several teachers that advise me on the overall improvements in a student's work and behaviours since they started

From the Classroom to the Sky – Aviation VET in School

learning to fly. Learning to fly helps you develop good habits and instills a sense of discipline and self-confidence when you achieve your flying milestones. These attributes are not something you think about when you first think of learning to fly, they are some of the added bonuses that can set you up for life.

If you know you want to be a pilot, this is the perfect way to get started. There are people that will tell you that if you want to do an Airline Cadetship or join the Air Force then you should not do any flying beforehand as you will jeopardise your chances. I do not believe this to be the case. I have taught pilots that are now RAAF pilots and Airline Cadet pilots. If anything, it is an opportunity to see if you really do like flying before signing up for significant time or financial commitment.

Learning to fly is a privilege and one to be grateful for. If you are at school and want to experience learning to fly, the Aviation VET programme is a means in which you can achieve this and, in some states, you are able to obtain a credit towards your end of year 12 score.

AFTERWORD

Time to Take Off

I knew from a young age that I wanted to be a pilot, and it has afforded me some extraordinary experiences for which I will be forever grateful. The students I have trained have forged their own paths in the aviation industry, flying all over the world. Now you understand more about what is required to become a pilot yourself, it is time for you to take the next step. You are armed with enough knowledge to ask the right questions to seek out the pathway that is right for you. Remember that knowledge is power, but only if you chose to use it. Be prepared to revisit this book after you have started your flying training, as different chapters will continue to assist you as you progress and are a valuable resource to return to.

I once read a book by Nancy Bird (Walton) called *My God, It's a Woman*, which helped me realise that many women have gone before me to make my path easier. In my life, I have been fortunate to have known Nancy personally and if, like her book, I can help to make your path a little smoother, it has made all of this worthwhile. It's time to take the next step and get into the left seat.

> "When once you have tasted flight, you will forever walk the earth with your eyes turned skyward, for there you have been, and there you will always long to return."
>
> – **Leonardo da Vinci**

CHAPTER 13
BONUS CHAPTER

A GLOBAL OPPORTUNITY – INTERNATIONAL STUDENTS

This book has been talking about learning to fly and learning to fly in the Australian system. If you are living outside of Australia, I would suggest that once you have read this chapter you read the remainder of the chapters in this book to get a greater appreciation of how learning to fly is achieved in Australia.

If you want to learn to fly in Australia and you are not a resident or citizen of Australia, you can do so, however you must first have the appropriate visa to study in Australia. If you are currently offshore and would like to study full-time to become a pilot, you should do this by going through a process of applying to become a student in Australia and obtaining a student visa. If you are able to live and possibly also work in Australia without a visa, there is no issue about learning to fly here. However, if you are required to have a visa and you plan to train for more than 12 weeks, noting that a

CPL programme lasts longer than this period, you will need to have a form of a student visa.

Finding a Flight School

To obtain a student visa, you need to learn to fly at an institution that is CRICOS registered. The CRICOS register is the Commonwealth Register for International Courses for Overseas Students. The flight schools that can offer these courses will be Registered Training Organisations. A university or TAFE college may also have courses for international students and be CRICOS registered. Understanding that not all flight schools have this registration will help narrow down the search for approved flight training schools.

After you have narrowed down your list of flight schools, you will need to select the city in which you wish to conduct your pilot training. This will help you decrease the number of flight schools on your list to only a handful. When you do look at the shortened list of flight schools, you are likely to find that most of the flight schools that are offering courses to overseas students are offering the CPL .

There are many reasons for this but the most common is that, if you're going to the trouble of obtaining a student visa, there is significant investment in time completing the forms to show you meet the requirements for the student visa, both for the applicant and the flight school. Going through the process for the PPL doesn't generally happen, but there is nothing stopping you.

The way the Australian system is designed, the courses on offer to international students in the pilot training space are required to be an award course, that is a course that acquires the academic title of certificate, diploma or advanced diploma, for example. This is why when you research you find that the piloting courses offered to international students are, at minimum, at the diploma level, the most common of which is the Diploma of Aviation Commercial Pilot Licence. For those who are looking at adding an instrument rating to the CPL they will also be enroling in the Diploma of Aviation instrument rating. Technically, whilst you may only be interested in the licence and rating, you will be receiving the added bonus of the dual diplomas.

Once you have chosen your flight school and the course in which you wish to enrol, you will need to enrol directly with the institution. Even if you are using an approved education agent your application to enrol in the course will be sent to the institution. After enroling with the flight school direct or via an approved agent, if accepted you will receive a letter of offer for a place on the course. If you chose to accept, you will then receive an electronic confirmation of enrolment. This confirmation of enrolment is a legal document that will be used along with your visa application information to obtain your visa in your home country. There are conditions when you are studying in Australia as an overseas student. There will be certain conditions you will have to meet to qualify for the issue of a visa, if you are not applying through an education agent the flight school is likely to be able to direct you to someone if you require additional assistance.

One condition is English language proficiency. To study in Australia, you will be studying in English, so it is important that you have a good command of the language. A requirement of the visa is an English Language test. The IELTS is the most commonly taken test which gives you a score in each of reading, speaking, listening, and writing with an overall score. For the student visa, 5.5 is a minimum score, however you will need to check with the institution you plan on studying at. Many aviation flight schools will have a minimum of 6.0 to 6.5 for the CPL courses.

There are some exceptions to needing the English test scores, I am not going to list them but for example if you are a citizen of the United Kingdom, United States, New Zealand, Canada or the Republic of

Ireland, this is one example of not requiring the test score. You should also note that in the content of your CPL training course there is also an aviation English language test, this is not to be confused with the IELTS that you needed for your visa. It is an aviation English language test that you will take in the process of your flying training.

Another requirement of studying in Australia is being able to show you can pay for the entire course and your associated living expenses for the duration of the course. The Australian Government has a set amount outlined per month that you need to show for living expenses.

Paying for the Course

There are no set payment requirements, as different flight schools will have different payment plans. Some may take all the money at the beginning of the course, and some may stagger it over intervals, for example 10 regular payments over the duration of the course.

When you receive the letter of offer, it will outline all the items you are paying for and the specific payment schedule. One of the items listed will be overseas Student Health Cover (OSHC), a mandatory government requirement that ensures that you are covered for general medical expenses whilst studying. Just like any insurance, you have it just in case, and hope that you will not be required to use it.

After you arrive in Australia and start your course, the flight school will also have some specific rules which if not adhered to, they could lead to the cancellation of your visa. You will be made familiar with these prior to joining the course. The course will be full-time, and attendance is monitored. Even with a full-time course, your student visa allows you to work for 20 hours per week. Most institutes permit you to do this. However, you will have to ensure that it does not interrupt your full-time studies. The aim of you coming to Australia is to study, and in this instance study to become a pilot, and once your studies are complete, the assumption is, you will return back to your home country with an Australian pilot licence.

Can You Use an Australian Pilot Licence in Another Country?

Yes, but if you are planning on working in your home country you will need to convert it to the licence of your home country. (there may be some exceptions, but this would be for you to determine). The most common practice is, if you came from China, Vietnam, Singapore, India or Sri Lanka, to use as examples, each of those countries will have their own National Aviation Authority, just as we have the Civil Aviation Safety Authority, and that regulator will stipulate a process for conversion.

The conversion process will usually involve some form of theory examination or examinations and a flight check relative to the licence or rating being converted. Different countries will have different rules and procedures. Whichever country you are coming from, you should check these rules before you even apply to fly in Australia, to ensure you are aware of what you need to do. Failing to do so could lead you to not meeting the appropriate requirements upon returning home with the Australian Licence.

A different country may have a different minimum hours requirement. For example, if you enrolled and completed an Australian Diploma of Aviation CPL course which is integrated and has 150 hours, you may now hold and Australian CPL but you may not have enough hours to meet the licensing requirements of your home country. This would be the case in India, as the DGCA (the CASA equivalent regulator) stipulate you need 200 hours for the CPL. Although, you hold an Australian CPL, you will not be able to convert that licence until you meet the 200-hour requirement. That is why it is important to check before you enrol into a course.

Medical Requirements

Each country has its own licence, and with it are its own medical requirements. The medical requirements come from an international standard however, each country adopts different methods and checks to meet the standard. Class 1 medicals are required for professional pilot licences ie CPL and above and Class 2 medicals for the PPL. If you are planning on a career as a pilot in your home country, it is important that you pass a Class 1 medical before you commence your pilot training abroad. Like the flying hours, the last thing you would want when you return home after all that training is to find out you don't meet the medical standards.

Support Services

When you are studying in a foreign country, everything is different, and it can take a little while to settle in. Most schools will have student support services, and they will look after any issues you may have. The bonus with flight training is you spend a lot of one on one time with your flight instructor, so they tend to become your first point of call if you face issues, and they can either help or direct you to the correct person to ask.

Don't be Surprised

In keeping with the purpose of this book, I have included some of the things I have observed with international students searching for a course.

When comparing courses, make sure you are comparing apples with apples – as in, no two courses will be exactly the same, but the core components of the courses will be.

- Flight hours - dual and solo
- Extra flying hours - dual and solo
- Examination costs
- Theory course cost
- Additional theory instruction
- Flight test costs
- Textbooks
- Documents and flight equipment
- Landing and airways charges

These costs should be outlined in your letter of offer, however because you have to be enrolled to receive this then it is important that you make sure you are aware of them before you enrol.

Where Do I Stay?

Australia is a very multicultural country with, so many international students having friends or relatives in the country before they arrive. Students are permitted to stay with friends or relatives during their stay if that suits their needs.

If you don't have anywhere that you can stay, don't worry. You will have been provided with information when you applied for your visa, and also shown that you have enough money to cover your living expenses. Some flying schools and institutes have their own accommodation or assist the student to find accommodation nearby. Some may utilise the services of an organisation called Homestay or similar where students from all around the world stay in people's homes. Families are able to choose to host an overseas student in their family home. You can opt for meals being included if you wish. It is a good way in which to become familiar with the Australian way of life, and you can ask your host family some of the questions you may have about settling into a new country. A student may decide to stay in this type of accommodation for a few months when they first arrive to adjust to their new environment. When they are feeling more confident, they may elect to move into more independent accommodation.

Flying in Australia

Earlier chapters provide information about the licence structure in Australia and how it can be used. The flying conditions in Australia are typically good, and Australia has a sound reputation when it comes to teaching pilots how to fly. I have travelled to many countries in the world and there is never any argument on the quality of the Australian Pilot Training system. The weather in Australia is favorable to flying, as we don't have snow other than in isolated mountainous areas in the southeast of the country. Australia is vast, and the airspace easy to access. We have a large population of aeroplanes and flights schools across the country. Australia also has good infrastructure for pilot training for both Australian and overseas students.

Do Your Research

I have been training international students for more than 20 years and have been fortunate enough to meet many of them in their home country before they made their decision to travel to Australia. I also now have the pleasure of seeing them thrive in their airline careers. I appreciate that, unlike being a student in Australia, you cannot just knock on the door of the flight school. However, you can still do your homework. Email the flight school any of your questions, they should be prepared to answer them if they want you as a student. If you are unsure, make an appointment time with them to call to discuss your doubts. This is a big investment in your life and future, and it is important for you to be clear on what is involved. You want to feel comfortable that you have made the right decision and that you are going to be looked after with respect to you flight training needs.

A Global Opportunity - International Students

If you are from overseas and looking at studying to be a pilot in Australia, this book provides you with an understanding of how the Australian system works, with details on the steps to apply to study in Australia. You, too, can become one of the many successful pilots who learnt to fly in Australia.

ADRIANNE FLEMING

From a young age, Adrianne Fleming knew she wanted to fly. Now, she is one of the 4% of female pilots flying professionally in Australia. After completing secondary school, Adrianne became the first woman to graduate with an Associate Diploma of Applied Science in Fire Technology, which would become a stepping-stone to her future career in a male-dominated industry.

Adrianne worked as an Airways Data Systems Officer in the Air Traffic Control (ATC) radar centre at Melbourne Tullamarine whilst studying towards her Commercial Pilot Licence. After obtaining her licence, she left the ATC centre to pursue a career as a full-time pilot and completed her instructor rating. She worked part-time as an instructor whilst pregnant with her first son. In August 1993, when her son was three months old, she and her husband Geoff started Tristar Aviation, a flying school and charter company based at Moorabbin Airport.

Over the past 27 years, Adrianne has held various state and national office positions in the Australian Women Pilots' Association, encouraging women to pursue their dreams in aviation. In 2012 she received the Nancy Bird Walton award for the most noteworthy contribution to aviation in Australia and Australasia, and in 2016 was honoured to be awarded the Order of Australia Medal for her services to the Aviation industry.

In December 2020 Adrianne was appointed by the Deputy Prime Minister to the Future of Aviation Reference Panel. She is a member of the CASA Aviation Safety Advisory Panel and also for 10 years held the positon of the Victorian Group Executive Commissioner of the Australian Air League, leading 13 cadet squadrons across the state. Adrianne has spearheaded the overseas marketing of Tristar Aviation throughout India, Sri Lanka, Vietnam, Bangladesh, Rwanda and, more recently, Indonesia. She travels regularly to market Tristar's courses and liaise with airlines and regulatory authorities to continually improve the pilot courses Tristar offers to international students. She has also been appointed to the board the Professional Airline Board of Certification, an international body aiming to improve pilot training globally.

Adrianne is currently the Head of Operations and CASA Flight Examiner for Tristar Aviation, working alongside her husband in pursuing her passion for aviation flight training, as well as raising two more children, firmly believing that blending flying and family is possible – and it works.

Speaker Topics

1. Women in aviation – how women are changing the face of the industry and what it takes to make it happen

2. Growing businesses while raising kids – how to build your empire while raising kids and managing a household

3. Sky-high business blueprint – the critical first two years of business and how to grow it successfully on a shoestring budget

4. Successful committees - empower your team to extend your not-for-profit (NFP) organisation's reach into the community

📞 +61 3 9580 6200   www.tristaraviation.com.au   ✉ adrianne@tristaraviation.com.au

CONCLUSION

This template is a guide only to enable you to see where costs are incurred and to put a price to each of them. The RPL and PPL are fairly straight forward. With the CPL, there are several ways in which to achieve the outcome.

Need Help?

If you want to book a 30-minute clarity session with me to unpack and discuss your options, please email adrianne@tristaraviation.com.au

The Left Seat

PRICING TEMPLATE

Download PDF from www.adriannefleming.com.au

This template is in 5 sections RPL, PPL CPL and Multi engine class rating and Instrument Rating (IR)

Completing this is a guide to what the price of obtaining the different Licences and ratings. It will allow you to compare apples with apples. Please make sure you read the notes in the instructions that relate to each * number when you are completing the table. You will need to print off one set for each flying school comparison. If you have questions after completing this my details are on the last page with my special clarity session offer.

Name of Flight School _____

Recreational Pilot Licence (RPL)

Aircraft Type	Cost per hour dual	x 20		1 *
Aircraft Type	Cost per hour solo	x 5		2
Medical Cost				3 *
Security ID ASIC/AVID				4 *
RPL Theory Course				5 *
CASA RPL Licence Issue				6 *
RPL Theory Exam				7
RPL Flight Test Examiner				8 *
Aviation English Language Assessment				9 *
RPL Flight Test Aircraft	Cost per hour (hire)	x 1.5 (approx.)		10
Pilot Headset				11 *
Miscellaneous Items				12 *
Total RPL (sum of lines 1 to 12)				13

Conclusion

Private Pilot Licence

Aircraft type	Cost per hour dual	x 20		14
Aircraft type	Cost per hour solo	x 5		15
PPL theory Course				16 *
PPL theory Exam				17 *
ASA Documents & publications				18 *
Navigation Charts				19 *
Navigation Equipment				20 *
Additional Landing Fees				21 *
PPL Flight Test Examiner				22 *
RPL Flight Test Aircraft	Cost per hour (hire)	x 2.5 (approx.)		23
CASA PPL Licence Issue				24
Total PPL (sum of lines 14 to 24)				25

Commercial Pilot Licence 150 hour integrated
Command Hours building to 150 hour integrated CPL *

Aircraft Type	Cost per hour solo	x 55	26 *

Commercial Pilot Licence 150 hour integrated training

Aircraft Type (Misc Training)	Cost per hour dual	x 12	27 *
Aircraft Type (Design Feature Training)	Cost per hour dual	x 5	28 *
Aircraft Type (CPL Training)	Cost per hour dual	x 20	29
Aircraft Type (CPL Training)	Cost per hour solo	x 5	30
CPL Theory Course (all 7 subjects)			31 *
CPL Exams (all 7)			32
CPL Flight Test Examiner			33
CPL Flight Test Aircraft	Cost per hour (hire)	x 3.5 (approx.)	34
CASA CPL Licence Issue			35
Total CPL Component (sum of lines 26 to 35)			36

Total for integrated CPL Sum 13+25+36			37

Conclusion

Commercial Pilot Non-integrated (200hour)
Command Hours building to 200 hour CPL

Aircraft Type	Cost per hour solo/hire	x 105	38 *

Commercial Pilot licence 200 hour CPL training

Aircraft Type (misc training)	Cost per hour dual	x 12	39 *
Design Feature Training	Cost per hour dual	x 5	40 *
Aircraft Type	Cost per hour dual	x 20	41
Aircraft Type	Cost per hour solo	x 5	42
CPL Theory Course All Subjects or			43 *
CPL Theory HUF			44 *
CPL Theory Navigation			45
CPL Theory Meteorology			46
CPL Theory Aerodynamics			47
CPL Theory Air Law			48
CPL Theory Aircraft General Knowledge			49
CPL theory Performance & Operations			50
CPL Exams (all 7)			51
CPL Flight Test Examiner			52
CPL Flight Test Aircraft	Cost per hour (hire)	x 3.5 (approx.)	53
CASA CPL Licence issue			54
Total CPL Component (sum of lines 38 to 54)			55

Total 200 hour CPL (sum 13+25+55)			56

The Left Seat

Multi-Engine Class Rating (MEA)

Aircraft Type	Cost per hour dual	x 5		57
MEA Flight Test Examiner				58
MEA Flight Test Cost Aircraft	Cost per hour hire	x 1.5		59
Total MEA Class Rating (Sum 57+58+59)				60 *

Instrument Rating (IR)

Simulator Type	Cost per hour dual	x 20		61 *
Aircraft Type	Cost per hour dual	x 20		62 *
Instrument Approach Charges/and Airways Charges	Cost per approach	Number of approaches		63 *
Instrument Rating Theory Course (IREX)				64 *
CASA IREX Examination				65
Instrument Rating Charts and Documents				66 *
IR Flight Test Examiner				67
IR Flight Test Aircraft	Cost per hour (hire)	x 2.5 (approx.)		68
Total IR (sum 61 to 68)				69

Note items - Please consider these items when you are completing the cost's in each of the boxes. This is a guide only and you should consult your flying school for final quotes and confirm GST applicability.

Note 1 The 20 hours is the minim number of hours (if inside an integrated course it could be 15 but don't price on this) With any hourly rates always check if there are landing fees and if they are included in the rate. If not, you will need to factor this into your calculations.

Note 3 Remember class 2 for Private flying and Class 1 for Commercial- the price will vary between DAMEs – be sure to check

Note 4 You will need a security check to gain a licence. Some airports will require an ASIC not AVID remember to ask which will be required for where you are training.

Conclusion

Note 5 RPL theory course, can be part time or full time, check whether it includes the exam and text book, if not you will need to add in the text book cost.

Note 6 Check to see if this was included with the course cost, if so don't count it twice

Note 8 There may be a rate for the flight test that includes the examiner check this or it may be called an examiner rate. It is likely the aircraft hire rate will be separate which is why I have included an additional line for this

Note 9 Aviation English Language is a requirement you need to satisfy to gain the licence, it is a separate recorded verbal test with an approved person.

Note 10 If there is a separate fee for the examiner and the test then you will need to pay for the aircraft separately, this is usually at the hire rate for the aircraft.

Note 11 Two way communication is required when you are learning to fly. Purchasing a headset is an important part of your toolkit. The flight school is likely to have some available for use for the early lessons but it is important you purchase your own.

Note 12 Miscellaneous items, this line is for any additional items that may be required by the flight school, for example a fuel tester, theory briefings or books

Note 16 PPL theory course, like RPL check to see if it includes the relevant text books and exam. If you chose to self study the theory then you may only need to put in the text book cost in this box

Note 17 PPL theory exam, this can be completed at the flight school or an exam centre. If completing a course check whether it is included in the fee.

Note 18 Air Services Australia documents, these may be included in your theory course. If so no need to include them in this box

Note 19 Navigation Charts- Depending on where you are learning to fly the number of charts required may vary

The Left Seat

Note 20 There are a few different varieties of equipment available for pricing it is comparable however when it comes to purchasing make sure you seek the guidance of your instructor before purchasing.

Note 21 In the PPL phase you may visit aerodromes that incur additional landing fees so be sure to factor these in if relevant

Note 22 As for the RPL the examiner may be included in what is listed as a test fee

Note 26 Hours building for the 150 hour integrated CPL these hours will be listed in specific aircraft type/s if more than 1 type you will need to add an additional line

Note 27 Miscellaneous training- this is most likely to be hours used to gain your RPL and PPL remember I quoted at the minimum hours which is rare so consider these hours a buffer.

Note 28 Design feature training- the CPL needs to completed in an aircraft with a MPPC I have included 5 hours for this training.

Note 31 CPL theory in the integrated course will likely include all 7 subjects, be sure to check if the text books and documents are inclusions in the course. Also check whether it includes the examinations

Note 38 The command hours for the non integrated (200 hour) CPL course is a minimum of 100. To keep the dual hours to the same as the integrated the amount of extra command hours comes to 105. Remember you can cost share these hours with others which can reduce the amount. You may also use a variety of aircraft for these hours to suit your purpose so you may need to add additional lines here.

Note 39 I have kept the miscellaneous hour the same as in the integrated course to compare as per note 26- this is most likely to be hours used to gain your RPL and PPL remember I quoted at the minimum hours which is rare so consider these hours a buffer.

Note 40 Design feature training- the CPL needs to completed in an aircraft with a MPPC I have included 5 hours for this training. (as per Note 27 in the integrated training)

Conclusion

Note 43 CPL theory subjects can be completed as an entire course or as separate subjects, check inclusions such at text books, documents and exams

Note 44 Any of the 7 CPL theory subjects can be self studied. If you select to do this you will still need to include the cost of the text book in lines 43-49

Note 60 There are some flight schools that may include the Multi engine class rating inside the training for the CPL (if so look at the hours and substitute in for some of the miscellaneous hours (line 26 or 38) and add in the flight test- It is possible the flight test may be combined with the CPL flight test if so the don't add in the aircraft flight test hours (line 58)

Note 61 There is a maximum of 20 hours instrument flight in the flight simulator that can be counted towards the instrument rating. As the simulator is generally more economical than an aircraft most people select to do this as a more affordable option.

Note 62 As part of your PPL you have 2 hours of instrument flying and CPL you may have up to 10 hours. These hours may be used towards your total however it will depend on your course as to what actual relevant experience you gained in that training. Instrument flight is when you are flying the aircraft soley by referent to instruments so if you completed a dual lesson of 2 hours you would not be able to log 2 hours instrument flight as there would be the taxiing on the ground etc. However 20 hours by the aircraft and including your previous instrument time should be enough to total the 20 hours you require.

Note 63 It will depend on what type of instrument approached you add to the instrument rating. The charges may be included in the dual hire or be listed separate for each flight as incurred.

Note 64 If the instrument rating theory may be self studied if so then only include the cost of the book

Note 65 Instrument rating Charts and documents, these will also be needed for the theory course whether you are self studying or not. If you are completing a course check to see if any of these are included.

Diploma and Degree cost

If you are undertaking a Diploma or a Degree there will be additional costs to these for the academic classes and assessments

Conclusion

This template is a guide only to enable you to see where costs are incurred and to put a price to each of them. The RPL and CPL are fairly straight forward. With the CPL there are several ways in which to achieve the outcome.

NEED HELP

If you want to book a 30 minute clarity session with me to unpack and discuss your options please email adrianne@tristaraviation.com.au

FURTHER TESTIMONIALS

"From my very first email enquiry, Adrianne guided me through the entire process of learning to fly. During my training she was always there to answer my questions and make sure that I was on track to achieve my goal. I am now an A320 captain and am forever grateful that it was Adrianne that answered that first email."

Capt Mohamed Dailami

"Adrianne Fleming, OAM, assisted me to set up the very successful Aviation Programme at our school, thus providing unique opportunities for our students. This informative book shows yet again Adrianne's passion for aviation and education."

Sabine Joseph
Director of STEM
Lyndale Secondary College

The Left Seat

"No matter how old you are flying is one of the most rewarding things you could do. It can be very confusing when you first start out. This book is a wonderful starting point. Learn from one of our most respected in the industry."

Deborah Evans
President
Australian Women Pilots' Association

"It is a great pleasure to recommend this well-researched and skilfully crafted book by aviator Adrianne Fleming, OAM. This book is a delight to read; it is full of perspectives and details that will smooth the way for future aviators."

Capt Jack Ekl
Boeing Instructor
Former Blue Angel

"Seeing and understanding how it all works and where to start, from the eyes of such a highly regarded and professional pilot, is truly wonderful. This is an easy read which gives you a sound knowledge of the challenges of flight training."

William Hurley
Pilot

"Having just been appointed the first female CEO of an Indian Airline, I find Adrianne's passion for aviation inspirational, as are her important honours and awards. She is a role model for young women to reach their dreams to become pilots and leaders in the aviation industry. This book is a must read for any person who wants to learn to fly under the Australian system."

Harpreet A De Singh
CEO Alliance Airlines
IWPA President

Further Testimonials

"Adrianne has a remarkably simple way of explaining the complexities of the flight training system without confusing jargon."

John Ballagh
Principal- Brentwood Secondary College

ABOUT THE AUTHOR

Adrianne Fleming is the author of *The Left Seat - Avoid the Turbulence on Your Journey to Becoming a Licensed Pilot*. She is co-owner and Head of Operations of Tristar Aviation, based in Melbourne, as well as being a Flight Instructor and Examiner. Adrianne's 30 years contributing to the aviation industry have generated a wealth of experience that she shares in this book for aspiring pilots.

Adrianne is the recipient of the prestigious *Nancy Bird Award for the Most Noteworthy Contribution to Aviation by a Woman in Australasia*, and in 2016 she was awarded an *Order of Australia Medal* for her Service to the aviation industry. She has worked with aviation regulators in Australia and overseas giving her a unique knowledge of more than one system of licensing.

In addition to her business and community responsibilities, Adrianne enjoys reading recipe books, experiencing new foods and cooking for family and friends. She has a weakness for sari shopping in India and has a colourful collection in her wardrobe.

USEFUL LINKS

Tristar Aviation Company Pty Ltd – www.tristaraviation.com.au

The Australian Air League - www.airleague.com.au

The Australian Women Pilots' Association – www.awpa.org.au

Women In Aviation International -Australian Chapter – www.waiaustralia.org

Honourable Company of Air Pilots - https://airpilots.org.au/

Australian Aerobatic Club - www.aerobaticsaustralia.com.au

Aircraft Owners and Pilots Association - https://aopa.com.au/

The Australian Beechcraft Society - https://abs.org.au/

The Cessna 182 Association of Australia - https://www.cessna182.org.au/

Australian Mooney Pilots Association - https://www.mooney.org.au

Recreational Aviation Australia - https://www.raa.asn.au/

Sport Aircraft Association - https://saaa.asn.au/

The Civil Aviation Safety Authority – www.casa.gov.au

Dr Sean Runacres (DAME) – https://www.saraviationmedicine.com.au/

www.ingramcontent.com/pod-product-compliance
Lightning Source LLC
Chambersburg PA
CBHW021438080526
44588CB00009B/589